MOST PEOPLE DON'T NEED A THERAPIST THEY JUST NEED A CHANGE

This raw and intimate look inside Monique's personal experience gives us all a blueprint for improving our own lives. What an enlightening read!

Michelle Wright, News Anchor

Most People Don't Need a Therapist, They Just Need a Change is a gift in a user-friendly format to all who seek to change their beliefs and behaviors. Monique offers step-by-step techniques to release negative beliefs, increase self-esteem, open to forgiveness of self and others, and experience empowerment in altering your life path. Coach Monique's intimate story of self-discovery supports and encourages the reader to believe that we all have the power within us to change.

Gail Hunter, ACSW, LCSW, BCD

Coach Monique's highly engaging book will inspire and lead readers to emotional health and overall well-being. Whether you are just starting on the path to greater happiness or are a veteran seeker, her techniques and practices provide valuable tools for the journey. Monique's encouraging words and thoughtful lessons gently guide the reader, while her life story illustrates her hard-won insight. The clear, organized approach makes this a book you will want to read and reread for years to come.

Anne Kertz Kernion, Owner of Cards by Anne

Coach Monique's very personal approach to self-awareness and improvement will be very helpful to the men and women facing divorce that I see in my family law practice. The end of a marriage is a complex and challenging time. Coach Monique provides right-on insights and helpful tools that will provide much needed support, which will in turn ensure a healthier more successful life transition.

Hilary A. Spatz, Esquire

If you want to replace negative thoughts, untie yourself from a painful past, and peel away false beliefs, this book will give you easy techniques manifesting in quick, visible results in your life. *Most People Don't Need a Therapist, They Just Need a Change* is THE book to read.

C. James Jensen, Author of 7 Keys to Unlocking Your Full Potential

This book by Coach Monique DeMonaco is exactly like her: educational, inspirational, and uplifting. Monique opens up about her own personal experiences and those of her clients, making herself someone to which you can relate. Her step-by-step instructions on meditation and positive thinking make her methods easy and understandable. For anyone who wants to undertake the task of self-improvement, but isn't sure how to do so, this book is a must-read.

Amy Hursh, MD, Family Medicine

Coach Monique has changed the way that I look at life. I have personally achieved my own inner smile and inner peace of mind. Monique is a deeply evolved soul who has enriched my world.

Dan Burda, Political Activist, and Co-Owner of Studio Raw and The Raw Hogs Media Company

As a physician, I see firsthand how a negative internal dialogue creates physical and emotional illness. Coach Monique outlines a simple yet powerful approach to reprogram how we deal with anger, stress, and self-doubt. Readers can easily incorporate her techniques into a busy and hectic schedule.

Amy K. Imro, MD, FACOG, NCMP

MOST PEOPLE DON'T NEED A THERAPIST, THEY JUST NEED A CHANGE

An Easy-to-Use Guide for Positive, Sustainable Change

Monique DeMonaco, MBA

MOST PEOPLE DON'T NEED A THERAPIST, THEY JUST NEED A CHANGE
AN EASY-TO-USE GUIDE FOR POSITIVE, SUSTAINABLE CHANGE
Copyright © 2015 by Monique DeMonaco

All rights reserved. No part of this publication may be reproduced, distributed, or transmitted in any form or by any means, including photocopying, recording, or other electronic or mechanical methods, without the prior written permission of the author, except in the case of brief quotations embodied in critical reviews and certain other noncommercial uses permitted by copyright law. Submit permission requests to the author, at the address below.

This book is designed to provide information and motivation to readers. It is sold with the understanding that the publisher is not engaged in rendering any type of psychological, legal, or any other kind of professional advice. The content is the sole expression and opinion of the author, not necessarily that of the publisher. No warranties or guarantees are expressed or implied by the publisher's choice to include any of the content in this volume. Neither the publisher nor the author shall be liable for any physical, psychological, emotional, financial, or commercial damages, including, but not limited to, special, incidental, consequential, or other damages. The author and publisher views and rights are the same: You are responsible for your own choices, actions, and results.

The Delete Delete™ Technique is a method developed by Monique DeMonaco.

Most People Don't Need a Therapist, They Just Need a Change™ is a title developed by Monique DeMonaco.

To contact the author, Monique DeMonaco, visit
   Website .... http://www.CoachMonique.com
   Email .... Monique@CoachMonique.com
   LinkedIn............... http://www.linkedin.com/in/moniquedemonaco
   Facebook............ https://www.facebook.com/pages/Coach-Monique/219837854829220

Printed in the United States of America.

To contact the publisher, inCredible Messages Press, visit http://www.inCredibleMessages.com.

ISBN 978-0-9889266-7-7 Paperback
ISBN 978-0-9889266-8-4 eBook

Book coach .... Bonnie Budzowski, inCredible Messages, LP
Cover design .... Bobbie Fox Fratangelo, Bobbie Fox, Inc.
Author photo.......... Courtney Halle Photography

DEDICATION

I dedicate this book to all the people who want change and are courageous enough to do what it takes.

> "Your life does not get better by chance, it gets better by change."
> - Jim Rohn

CONTENTS

Acknowledgments I
An Invitation to Positive Life Change 1
My Journey from There to Here—How I Know This Stuff Works 11
When You Change Your Thoughts, You Change Your Life......................... 27
Everyone Self-Soothes—Your Self-Soothing Doesn't Have to Hurt 39
You Have Power to Shift Your Body, Mind, and Energy
To a Better Place Whenever You Need To 53
The Story You Tell Yourself Is Just a Story—Make It a Good One! 65
Feelings and Intention Attract—Make Your Focus Positive 75
Your Heart Has Transformative Power—Cultivate Heart
Intelligence to Access That Power... 87
Talking and Communicating Are Different Things—Make Sure You
Are Communicating 93
Backsliding Is Inevitable—Step into the Next Best Version of
Yourself to Keep Facing Forward 109
Forgiveness Is the Gift You Give Yourself... 121
Cap It Off with Confidence.. 133
Good-bye for Now—A Few Closing Words 149
Ready Reference Guide for Easy-to-Learn, Easy-to-Use, and
Immediately Relevant Techniques 155
About the Author 159

Acknowledgments

Although I'm the author of this book, in many ways I am not the inventor. I've been the recipient of wisdom, compassion, insight, and love from many sources. I am grateful for the help I've received in completing my own inner work, the authors and teachers who have taught me, and family members who have loved and accepted me.

The information in this book is distilled or adapted from all the education and training I have had. For example, I didn't invent meditation; literally hundreds of mediation methods are out there. I simply designed a method that I feel fits the framework: easy-to-learn, easy-to-use, and immediately relevant.

I'm also not the first person to say your thoughts have power or that forgiveness is essential for true happiness. I simply formatted information and created techniques to help you get rapid results so you can move on with your life—healthier, happier, more relaxed, and at peace to have the *changes* that are important to you.

I have been fortunate to have worked with some great therapists: Gail Hunter, Amanda Thomas, Kirsten Bolt, Thad Ryan, and Edy Ryan. From them I learned: It's my job to love myself; self-care is not selfish; change what I can, accept what I can't, and know the difference; and to make the hard choices and let go as a parent.

Some of the great authors and experts (I could never list them all), who have helped shape the person I am today through their writings include Thich Nhat Hanh, Rick Hanson, Ph.D., Michio Kaku, Robert Holden, Ph.D., Caroline Myss, Candace Pert, Ph.D., Brené Brown, Ph.D., Daniel J. Siegel MD, Gregg Braden, Bryon Katie, Eric Butterworth, Don Miguel Ruiz, and Bruce Lipton, Ph.D. I have benefitted immensely. Thank you.

In addition, programs such as Silva, Landmark Education, and Open Sky have been rich resources of ideas, processes, and support to me.

Dan Burda, thank you for all your creativity, support, and encouragement. Your ideas about my trademark bejeweled Coach's Whistle, Coach Monique's Friday Confessional, and your endless marketing and promotional insights have helped me reach full-time success much sooner than I would have otherwise. I love my time in the "Magic Chair" as you keep my hair current. You are a wise and beautiful man.

Mary Jo Biceglia-Tilves, thank you for all the "cheerleading" and willingness to be "Red Pen Ready." Your editing skills and objective advice give me the confidence to publish my voice each week whether it is in blog or book. You are also a loving friend who has consistently supported our family, even when it meant more work for you. I take comfort having you in our lives.

Bonnie Budzowski, thank you for taking this book project and me on, particularly when I announced that I wanted to complete a project in 5 months that can typically take up to 18 months to do. Your guidance, insights, organization, and editing helped ensure this was a book of excellence. You are the consummate professional and writing coach.

Brandon Firman, thank you for so much for so many things. From technical support late into the night, to using your creativity at crunch time, to putting together all the audio downloads for this book, you have saved the day on more than one occasion and have simply been a joy and a pleasure. Some of my fondest memories when reflecting back on this summer will be having you, Lauren, and Anso provide me with a much needed break in the middle of the night when the "right" word was escaping me or I just needed some company. You have quickly become like another son. I look forward to what I hope is a life-long friendship.

Thank you to my dear "Chatham Friends," Kathi, Mary Jean, Louise, JoAnn, Cheri, and Beverly. What started out as lunch in the cafeteria has become 25 years of wonderful friendship. While our group has expanded and changed over the years, you have remained my dearest friends and biggest supporters. You have seen me through some of my most painful struggles (losing my grandparents and divorce) and celebrated me with wedding and baby showers. You supported me in my family and career adventures. Our monthly dinners provide a sense of connection, laughter, inspiration, and love. I wish you all only the best life has to offer. I love you.

Larry, I love you the "mostess" and always will. You came into the boys' and my life when the days were pretty dark. You brought light, love, laughter, and a sense of commitment with you that most other men could never imagine. You are an amazing dad to the boys and a supportive husband to me. Thank you for keeping the home fires burning so I can have a career that I previously only dreamed of.

Scott, as my first born, you and I, in many ways, grew up together. It seems like just yesterday was the first day of school for both of us. My only regret is that I was not always the mother you deserved. Know that I love you more than words can say and am proud of the man you have become.

Anso, words cannot express the respect I have for the work you have done in your life already. You have had the courage to do what some men three times your age simply would not do, and I sincerely hope you continue down that path. Having you home the summer I wrote this book made the whole thing so much sweeter—welcome home. I love you, Anso.

Henry, your smile lights up a room. Your hard work and dedication make me so proud. Being your mom brings me so much joy. I love you.

Zane, your "thinking outside of the box," tenacity, and creativity inspire me. Your liveliness fills a room. I am lucky to have you as a son. I love you.

Mom, thank you for supporting the boys and me through some of our darkest days. I know that you love me, and I hope you know that I love you and always will. May you always have happiness in your heart.

Eric, although I don't say it enough, I love you and have so much respect for the wonderful life and family you have built. Luci, thank you for making Eric such a happy man. I love you both.

CHAPTER 1

AN INVITATION TO POSITIVE LIFE CHANGE

A KEY INDICATOR OF YOUR SUCCESS and happiness is the quality of the Voice in Your Head. This is true because wherever you go, whatever you do, and with whomever you associate, that Voice in Your Head has a powerful grasp on your attention, feelings, and perceptions. If the Voice in Your Head tells you that you are a winner, you'll act in ways that prove the Voice right. If the Voice in Your Head tells you that you are a loser, you'll act in ways that prove the Voice right.

I use the term *Voice in Your Head* to refer to the streaming, run-of-the-mill thought process nearly all of us experience. I refer to the Voice that criticizes, bitches and moans, judges, worries, complains, projects into the future, regrets the past, is sometimes mean, and is sure that you and others are flawed in important ways. This internal Voice stresses you out, focuses on what you don't have, repeatedly points out what is wrong, and insists you will always stay "stuck."

When I speak of the Voice in Your Head, I am not talking about a voice that screams obscenities, directs people to hurt themselves or others, and causes destruction and chaos. If you experience that kind of voice, seek immediate medical help. This book is not meant for you, at least not now.

I used to think the unhappy Voice in My Head was peculiar to me—that I had the negative Voice because I deserved it. After all, I was flawed, incompetent, burdened, and had plenty of real reasons to worry.

Then, one day, while waiting for my son's dismissal from a school event, I listened to a large group of parents discussing the challenges of their lives. Their voices were full of frustration, anger, worry, and a sense of burden. The parents all seemed stressed; they all seemed low on the happiness continuum.

As I listened, I was struck by how, from any objective standpoint, this group was well off. Although I didn't know the details of their lives, I felt confident that few, if any, of these upper-middle-class people were losing their homes, facing devastating financial woes, or dealing with tragic life-or-death issues. However, no one would have confused this group with a happy one. Most blamed spouses, kids, or in-laws for their problems. Some blamed the demands of their careers, and some simply lamented how "hard life is." As I listened that day, I had an epiphany: If members of this group couldn't be happy, what chance did the average person have?

The complaining internal voices of these parents were projecting negative words into their speech. The negative words were reinforcing the negative voices in their heads in a downward spiral. It almost seemed as if there were an unspoken competition for who got the Poor Me Prize. The lucky winner would get to wear the prize like a badge of honor. The whole interaction was steeped in the negative, but no one seemed to be aware of it.

This experience had a profound impact on me because I had battled with my own unhappiness. I had invested in training, education, and therapy. In the process, I had come to understand that change is an inside job and had even become a geek in all things involving inner change. For some time during the process, I still assumed my unhappiness was largely rooted in my difficult childhood experiences. I had grown up feeling poor, with undiagnosed learning disabilities that made school torturous, and an undiagnosed seizure disorder that caused those around me to think of me as an inattentive, lazy daydreamer.

That day, while waiting for my son, the encounter with the unhappy group reinforced what I had begun to see years earlier: that unhappiness is almost never situation dependent; in fact, unhappiness is rooted in negative thoughts and beliefs about self, relationships, and reality. Most people spend their energy and resources on trying to change circumstances or other people—things outside themselves—in an effort to experience happiness on the inside. Chances are that the parents I overheard weren't even cognizant that they could develop awareness of their thoughts and learn skills to help them be more positive and happier. What's more, this group of parents could represent all kinds of people in all stations of life.

I could see that so many others, often seemingly successful people, were like me before I had begun inner change work: stressed, struggling, unhappy, feeling as if they didn't matter, and miserable in their relationships. Seemingly successful people were experiencing an emptiness they could not fill with trips to the mall, serial relationships, vacation destinations, and mindless activities designed to help them feel and do better. Such people seemed to feel as if their happiness, success, or love lives would come in the future. Meanwhile, today was full of struggles.

Reflecting on these truths, I realized also that most people are not interested in an in-depth study of the science of the mind as it pertains to changing their thoughts and behaviors, as I am. Many people, if not most, want change, but they have neither the interest nor the inclination to explore, in detail, how to get it. Most people want rapid increases in their happiness but aren't sure how to get it or even where to look.

In reflecting on what I heard from parents waiting to pick up their kids, I discovered my life's work. I intuitively knew that, if I developed easy-to-learn, easy-to-use, and immediately relevant tools, techniques, and education to help people make positive, sustainable changes, the work would make a difference not only in the lives of others, but in my own life. Suddenly I knew my years of seeking, studying, comparing, contrasting, and researching—all the work I had done for myself—could help others in much the same way that the work had helped me. Although the average person wasn't going to spend years doing what I had done, that person would gladly spend a few weeks, or even a couple of months, learning how to make sustainable changes in order to be happier.

I spent the next year pursuing a coaching certification in the field of emotional intelligence and reviewing all the healing work I had completed while pursuing my own health and happiness. Over the years, I had attended and completed thousands of hours of training related to meditation, mindfulness, personal growth, self-help, psychology of happiness, brain health, and spirituality. I had researched, read, and studied hundreds of books and programs on those and related topics. It now became my goal to review, revise, and meld everything I had learned, and was continuing to learn, to develop a fresh, innovative, and relevant approach for the average person who wanted to be happier, more peaceful, and more fulfilled in life.

I kicked off my first four-week series, Positively Life Changing, in a Pilates studio in my community. Eight people participated. Shortly after, I was asked to do a motivational speech at a retreat, and from there a director at a local college asked me to teach my Positively Life Changing at her school. I went on to teach Putting Out the Fire of Fear and A Happier You there as well. Over the years, the work has grown and expanded to my Most People Don't Need a Therapist, They Just Need a Change™ four-week series, one-on-one coaching, and employee development training, with a focus on flexibility for my clients.

My intuition was right: When you offer easy-to-learn, easy-to-use, and immediately relevant training for real and sustainable change, people see the value for themselves, their friends and family, and even their employees and teams. My work has evolved over the years. Ensuring that the work is fresh, innovative, engaging, and sometimes fun for my students and clients remains a priority. The responses I get let me know I am doing the work I was meant to do; it has value and makes a difference in people's lives.

For example, it is common for students to sign up for a four-week series and then ask to switch to private one-to-one coaching after the first class. Students do this because they can already see how powerful the work is. Parents send their children. Business owners, bosses, and team leaders give employees the gift of this work as part of their employee training and development. This book came about because so many workshop participants and clients said, "Please write a book. I want to be able to give the book to others and refer to what I've learned when I need it."

FRAMEWORK FOR HOW TO USE THIS BOOK

First, I want to say what this book is *not*. It is not therapy or a replacement for therapy! High-quality therapy can and does change lives. Therapy has helped me make major positive changes in my life on more than one occasion. In my opinion, a good therapist is worth his or her weight in gold—a not-so-good therapist, not so much.

This book *is* about education, tools, techniques, insights, and strategies that helped me make positive, sustainable changes. Now I want to share them with you. I've discovered (when working with a great therapist or working alone) that most of the work to make real sustainable changes in life happens while you are actually out there living your life—relating to loved ones, driving your car, cleaning your house, and struggling to make your life work. This book is designed to give you the tools to use, no matter what you are doing, to make major, positive, and sustainable changes. Some of the changes will be little ones that add up to big ones. Some of the changes will be big ones right out of the gate!

I have met very few people who are so blissfully happy that they don't want to make some changes in their lives. This book can help you make those changes. The material in this book was born out of the very best education, tools, techniques, and strategies that helped me make major changes in my life. I continue to use these tools and strategies even as I sit writing today.

Chapters 1 and 2 of this book set the stage for those that follow. You are just completing Chapter 1, which provides a high-level overview of how this book can guide you to complete the inner work that leads to increased happiness and a fuller life.

Chapter 2, My Journey from There to Here—How I Know This Stuff Works, provides a context for specific techniques. It provides highlights of my story and describes how these techniques have worked for me.

Each of the next chapters focuses on a particular subject and includes one or more techniques to help you make changes based on that subject matter. In most chapters, I have distilled volumes of information to offer material that is clear-cut, easy-to-understand, and relevant. The goal is not to go deep and turn you into an expert on any particular topic (except yourself), but to provide you with education, tools, techniques, and strategies you can use to achieve rapid results for real change in your life.

In Chapter 3, When You Change Your Thoughts, You Change Your Life, you will learn to become more aware of your thinking and thought patterns so you can begin to make subtle yet powerful changes in your thinking, the bedrock of success and happiness in life. You'll learn the Delete Delete™ Technique, a powerful method to transform negative into positive thoughts.

In Chapter 4, Everyone Self-Soothes—Your Self-Soothing Doesn't Have to Hurt, you will learn to identify and address negative self-soothing practices you currently use. You will learn to replace negative practices with positive self-soothing. New methods will be available when you are feeling stressed, anxious, worried, lonely, overwhelmed, or tired. In this chapter, you'll learn the Simple Meditation Technique, based on muscle-mind memory. You can complete this meditation in 20 minutes. In addition, you'll learn the On-Demand Relaxation Technique. This technique allows you to program your body to respond to a cue to relax.

In Chapter 5, You Have Power to Shift Your Body, Mind, and Energy to a Better Place Whenever You Need To, you will learn the Inner-Smile Technique. This technique allows you to capture and optimize your happiest moment in life so you can intentionally shift your thoughts, emotions, and energy to a better place anytime, anywhere, and under any conditions. You'll program your body to respond to a cue that you want to shift from a negative mental place to the place of your happiest moment.

In Chapter 6, The Story You Tell Yourself Is Just a Story—Make It a Good One, you will learn to tease out fact from fiction in your internal monologue. You'll learn that many of the things you accept as fact are actually just beliefs. Some of your "facts" even date back to your early childhood, the time before your logical mind had developed. These facts are actually the beliefs of the adults in your life at that time. You simply absorbed the beliefs as fact and, today, they remain largely unexamined. You'll learn the Peel-Away-the-Story Technique, which will allow you to discover the core beliefs that drive your behavior and reality. You'll discover that you can change your story and, in the process, change your life.

In Chapter 7, Feelings and Intention Attract—Make Your Focus Positive, you'll explore the power of intention. You'll learn the Setting-an-Intention Technique, which will allow you to focus your thoughts and feelings to achieve or receive what you desire. Although people often set an intention to receive material goods, you'll learn that setting an intention can be deeper and more powerful than material goods.

In Chapter 8, Your Heart Has Transformative Power—Cultivate Heart Intelligence to Access That Power, you'll learn the Heart-Centered Breathing Technique. This technique will guide you to use your breath and visualization to shift your body chemistry and energy to states that are more positive.

In Chapter 9, Talking and Communicating Are Different Things—Make Sure You Are Communicating, you will learn that the quality of your relationships is one of the biggest indicators of success and happiness. Effective communication is the foundation of relationship success. In this chapter, you will learn multiple techniques and formulas to communicate effectively, even during the most trying times.

In Chapter 10, Backsliding Is Inevitable—Step into the Next Best Version of Yourself to Keep Facing Forward, you will learn to plan for setbacks and recognize obstacles before they become problems. The Stepping-into-the-Next-Best-Version-of-Yourself Technique will help to ensure your changes are sustainable.

In Chapter 11, Forgiveness Is the Gift You Give Yourself, you will learn how forgiving yourself as well as others is a critical step to becoming unstuck and moving toward the peace and happiness you desire. To be human is to make mistakes, sometimes unintentionally and sometimes intentionally. To be human is to be hurt by others, sometimes deservedly and sometimes undeservedly. The price of holding onto the hurt is a painful bondage. You'll learn the Forgiveness Technique and walk through the steps needed to break the bonds of anger and resentment. Forgiveness isn't easy, but it is essential.

In Chapter 12, Cap It Off with Confidence, you will learn quick pick-me-up strategies to get on-the-spot boosts of confidence. You'll identify guideposts to what it takes to become profoundly more confident from the inside out so that you can realize your goals and dreams today and for many tomorrows to come.

HERE IS WHAT YOU HAVE TO DO

- Actively participate as you read. Change doesn't get much easier than the work laid out in this book, but there aren't any shortcuts. You will get out of the book what you put into it.
- The first time through, read the book in sequence and in its entirety. The foundational material is in the early chapters. Digesting these chapters will allow you to have a solid foundation as you move through the chapters into topics that are more complex.
- While you are reading, learning, and doing the techniques, pay attention to how the work affects your life. Notice changes you experience, insights, and even dreams you may have.
- The work you do with this book will ripple out to all the areas in your life. Be on the lookout for how you are changing and how circumstances in your life begin to change. Almost every client I work with comes with a particular goal or set of goals. Clients quickly report that they see changes in other, seemingly unrelated, areas. The truth is, everything is related, so expect to see evidence of that and reap the rewards.

- Keep a journal to accompany this book. If formal journaling isn't your thing, at least take and keep notes.
- After you've completed the book, refer back to it. This book is designed to be a long-term resource, available when needed. Everyone needs a reminder or brush-up once in a while. Keep the book nearby and, when you find yourself struggling, return to the chapters that are pertinent to your issues at hand.
- Have fun and enjoy this process. At the initial training where I began this work myself, I literally felt a shift that ran into my core. Those first steps were exhilarating because of all the possibilities that suddenly opened up for me. This work can be exhilarating for you as well.

Chapter 2

My Journey from There to Here—
How I Know This Stuff Works

I used to have so many issues that I had to show up in life with a U-Haul. For example, on the morning of my first day of kindergarten, I woke up feeling sick. Mom said it was "just nerves." I went to school, and after meeting Mrs. Broomer, I told her I was sick. Mrs. Broomer said it was "just nerves." I promptly threw up and spent the next few days in bed with the flu. School was downhill from there.

Unbeknownst to my teachers, my parents, and me, I had significant learning disabilities that included working and auditory memory deficits. Although I may have been interested in what the teacher was saying, even a few seconds later I might not have been able to recall what it was. In addition, I lacked age-appropriate body and spatial awareness. Everything, from handwriting to gym, was a nightmare. To top it off, I had undiagnosed petit mal epilepsy. What appeared to be frequent bouts of daydreaming were actually seizures.

I grew up hearing mantras such as *you are lazy, you don't pay attention,* and *you make everything harder than it has to be,* spoken at both school and home. To say I just got by would be a gross understatement. For example, beginning in third grade and continuing through sixth grade, I spent hundreds of hours trying desperately to learn the multiplication tables. I simply could not learn them. No amount of rewriting, memorizing, or screaming made a difference. At age 28, I graduated from college still not knowing the multiplication tables. The same was true with states' names and capitals, parts of speech, and a myriad of other basics. Even today, I do not know the capital of Iowa or how to identify a dangling participle. The difference is that now I don't care!

Growing up, I lived in terror of failing a grade, not only because of the potential humiliation, but because school was such a brutal experience. I knew I simply could not extend my stay.

I lived in a time and in communities where bullying was rampant and tolerated; mean girls could literally kick your ass in class and not much was done about it. I was an easy target, frequently confused and often lacking direction. My homework was usually not done, and I had zero self-esteem.

Having my stuff vandalized—from having the buttons pulled off my coats in third grade to having my long denim coat, my beloved denim duster, stuffed into the toilet in middle school—reinforced the message that I was a loser who couldn't even have nice things. I endured the physical pain of being slammed into lockers as well as having my tailbone cracked when my chair was pulled out from under me, right as I sat down. To say I was a mess is a generous understatement.

I remember the humiliation when my middle school guidance counselor informed me I couldn't sign up for Spanish. Although a foreign language was necessary to go to college, the counselor said, "You don't get good-enough grades in English to be allowed to study Spanish. Besides, you aren't going to college, so it doesn't matter what classes you take." No matter where I turned, I was reminded of what a loser I was and how things weren't likely to change for me.

Although my parents loved me, I didn't feel particularly hopeful or happy at home. Mom, a beautiful Mensa genius, did not have the wherewithal to fathom why everything had to be so hard for me. Mom was busy struggling with her own issues of depression and a painful family history that haunted her.

Probably because of his own learning disabilities, Dad had suffered various types of abuse at home and at school. When Dad completed 10th grade, he decided to make a better life for himself. He "escaped" to the Marine Corps and Vietnam, long before the average U.S. citizen could find Vietnam on a map. The Marines and Vietnam only made things worse, and Dad returned more scarred than when he had left.

Chapter 2
My Journey from There to Here—How I Know This Stuff Works

Dad married, worked hard, and did his best to raise my brother and me, but eventually past wounds caught up with him. One hot summer day, Dad became seriously ill at work, was hospitalized, and couldn't work for an extended period. It was as if Dad had left for work one man and was delivered back to us a completely different one.

From that point on, Dad struggled with anxiety, stress, and anger. He was deeply mired in his own family's history of abuse and neglect. A downward financial spiral ensued. Before it was over, our family had lost our home, had taken a major step down on the socioeconomic ladder, and lost our ability to help or support one another through difficult times.

I grew up lonely, feeling poor, and sure I was not only dumb, but didn't matter. I saw myself as a loser and had no role models to demonstrate a better way. The Voice in My Head was definitely not my friend. The Voice ensured that I knew I was the ugliest, dumbest girl around. Unconsciously, I had integrated my childhood experiences into a story about who I was and what was possible for me. It would be many years before I questioned the validity of that story. Until I did, the story would drive my expectations, choices, behavior, and relationships.

I struggled through high school, and at 19 found myself married and with my first son, Scott. The marriage, as you might have guessed, didn't last. Although I didn't expect a whole lot for myself, I did have expectations and dreams for Scott. That marriage did not fit my ideal, so I ended it. At age 21, I was a divorcing single mother.

The next seven years held major life changes. I met Joe, the man who would become my second husband, and he introduced me to a whole new world. Joe lived in a world of college-educated professionals who lived in nice homes, drove new cars, ate at restaurants that required reservations, and had kids who participated in extracurricular activities. It struck me that, despite having everything I had not had in my life, few of these people seemed happy. In fact, most of these people seemed to be struggling with serious issues, such as unhappy or abusive relationships, low self-esteem, and addiction. Some even seemed tormented by life itself.

Joe claimed to see something in me that no one else had ever seen. He would tell me I was his "diamond in the rough." I certainly didn't see what he saw, but Joe treated me in ways that allowed me to be vulnerable on a new level. I vividly remember having one of the most profound conversations of my life with Joe. I told him I wished I were a smoker.

Appalled, Joe responded, "Why would you ever wish to be a smoker? People who smoke want to quit."

I explained my thinking: "If I were a smoker, I could choose to make a positive change and quit smoking." Irrational and stupid, I know, but that statement revealed my deepest, most vulnerable feelings. Because of that conversation and Joe's generosity, I ended up doing the unthinkable: going to college! At Joe's suggestion, I applied and was accepted to Chatham College, a local women's college.

At the time, Chatham College was struggling financially and experiencing low enrollment, so the school may not have had its most rigorous standards for incoming students in place. Knowing this, I spent my first year looking over my shoulder, fearing that someone would recognize that I didn't measure up. I expected to be asked to leave. I'm grateful it never happened, because good things ensued.

Although I graduated from college still not knowing the multiplication tables, I did get an amazing education. Some of my education was intellectual, but most was deeper and more important. It turns out that, although I was no Mensa genius, I could read, write, think, and present my work in ways that others not only respected, but wanted to hear. An intellectual curiosity and passion for lifelong learning was born. No one was more surprised than I was. You simply cannot imagine my sense of relief, gratitude, and excitement about having smarts.

At Chatham, I began to realize that my personal history did not have to decide my future. For the first time in my life, I met women doctors, attorneys, and executives who had received amazing educations at Chatham and kept strong ties with the college years after graduating. Many had overcome serious social issues, such as segregation and overt discrimination, and had become successful despite their obstacles.

Meeting these women, I began to realize that opportunity always exists. In addition I realized that opportunity favors those who believe something better is possible, are highly motivated, and are willing to sacrifice. Until that point, I had seen myself as a victim of circumstance. I was raised to believe my best opportunity to change my circumstance would come if I was lucky enough to marry a man with means. The idea that I could provide for myself had never occurred to me. Such an idea was not discussed in my family.

While at Chatham, I began to recognize that certain underlying beliefs my family held might be faulty. Among the beliefs were "People like us don't graduate from college; they have jobs, not professions, and they don't really have choices." I began to see that not only could I have and do better for myself, but that the same had been true for my parents and grandparents before me.

I struggled as I realized that my mother, in spite of her intelligence, hadn't chosen to step forward and work to support our family when my father had his breakdown. Suddenly, I saw Mom's behavior as a choice rather than the hand of fate that we, as a family, had simply accepted.

I began to see that I too had choices, starting with the opportunity to embrace the belief that I had choices. In short, I began to change the story I told myself about the past and the one I told myself about possibilities for my future. The transformation of my thoughts was by no means complete, but it had begun.

At 28, two months after graduating from college and after seven years of dating, I married Joe. I felt ready for the next chapter in my life. Within a few short years, I had a second son, Anso, and the ideal "curb appeal" life, one I had only dreamed about. I was now the proud mother of two, with the promise of more on the way. Joe ran a successful business that afforded us a beautiful home on a prestigious street, opportunity to travel, and a bustling social life. Life should have been great, right? Wrong! I was miserable.

I remember asking myself, "Is this all there is?" Although I loved Joe, the boys, and my family, a connection seemed missing. I was easily frustrated, and I often felt depleted in my relationships. I was often lonely and struggled with underlying unhappiness and insecurity.

I often chastised myself for not being happier. I felt ashamed that I wasn't. After all, during most of my life, I had had little financial security, let alone luxury. I had felt like a loser and lived in an environment of abuse and chaos. For so long I had felt as though I had few resources to make real change in my life. Now here I was, with a life I had expected to ensure happiness and security, and I was still miserable. Once again my thinking had been faulty. External things have no power to make a person happy. Happiness is an inside job.

One Christmas Day, I got a nudge that would put me on the path that would lead to my U-Haul getting significantly lighter. The path would lead me to finding more connection, love, happiness, success, self-acceptance, and self-love than I thought possible. Ultimately, the path would lead to my career as a coach and this book that you are holding.

It was a typical Christmas Day for us. My mom and stepfather, Jose, were staying with us. Santa had delivered the gifts, and the wrapping paper had been cleared away. I had successfully pulled off what I thought was a nice holiday brunch. Shortly after, everyone went along his or her merry way to a post-brunch nap or to explore the gifts. I found myself with a free hour until it was time to prepare for more festivities later in the day.

In that hour, I was shocked to find myself feeling pissed and lonely. I didn't know why because I love family and Christmas, and I was now in my dream home with the 12-foot bedazzling tree I had always thought was the hallmark of a perfect Christmas. My feelings simply didn't make sense to me.

Chapter 2
My Journey from There to Here—How I Know This Stuff Works

Feeling confused and ashamed, I reached for a small gift book lying on the table. Reading had always provided me an escape when I was hurting. I no longer remember the book or even the passage, but I remember a reference to a human potential training program in which the author had participated. The author talked about how the program had changed her life and how she still was grateful many years later.

As someone who had never seen the words *human, potential,* and *training* strung together, I was intrigued. Late that evening, after I had chastised myself for falling short on the Martha Stewart–style holiday dinner, I fired up the new computer Santa had delivered, to see what I could find. During my search that night, I found references to books and programs that seemed to hold promise for the kind of change I was beginning to suspect I needed.

The next morning, I scurried to the local bookstore to buy as many relevant books as they had in stock. To my delight, there were lots under headings such as Personal Growth, Self-Help, Spirituality, and Motivation. This visit to the bookstore was the beginning of a 10-year path I refer to as The Decade of Working Myself Like a Full-time Job. In that decade, I read hundreds of books and attended thousands of hours of programs, classes, workshops, seminars, and retreats.

I found myself giddy with excitement about what was possible. I began the work of becoming happier, healthier, and more peaceful as well as a better wife, mother, daughter, and friend. It was, and continues to be, a powerful emotional, spiritual, physical, and relational journey. Although often not easy and sometimes downright ugly, this journey has always been worth traveling.

I discovered that not only am I a geek when it comes to this stuff, but I am intellectually curious about and spiritually motivated to continue learning. I also enjoy the challenge of making it all work together. In short, I discovered my life's work.

I became more and more convinced that both happiness and change are inside jobs. If I wanted a better life for myself and my family, it was up to me to change from the inside out. It was time to set blame aside and take responsibility for the things I had power to control: my thoughts, beliefs, and behaviors.

When it came to examining my thoughts and beliefs, I had my work cut out for me. Although my success at Chatham had begun to alter my self-perception, I still had strong beliefs that I was incompetent at best and at worst, dumb. I had an ingrained perception of myself as a powerless victim, buffeted by circumstances and the choices of others. These thoughts had dictated how I saw myself, so I had low expectations for the possibilities open to me. Looking back, I could see clearly where I had quit trying to succeed. I had quit in high school because I believed success wasn't a possibility for me. I believed my efforts didn't matter.

As I studied after college, I discovered that there are multiple types of intelligence. Memorization, numbers, and test taking represent areas of struggle for me. However, emotional intelligence, social intelligence, linguistics, and interpersonal intelligence are clear strengths.

I began to see that no set of strengths and weaknesses is better than another and that no particular set guarantees success. This new, more accurate belief broadened my horizons and gave me a boost of confidence I had not experienced before. As wonderful as that was, I caught a glimpse of something even more dramatic.

I could see that, because I had always believed I wasn't good enough and didn't matter, I expected people to treat me as if I didn't matter. What's more, the lens of my expectation determined my interpretation of their behavior toward me. All my life, I had "seen" everywhere the evidence that I didn't matter. I saw it in the extreme experiences in my life, from being bullied in school to everyday irritations, such as being kept waiting or being interrupted. For example, if someone kept me waiting, the incessant Voice in My Head would declare, "If I mattered, this person would be more considerate." If someone said a rude or careless remark, the Voice in My Head would run the tape "You're not smart, and this person knows it."

Chapter 2
My Journey from There to Here—How I Know This Stuff Works

With such beliefs and self-talk, life wasn't much fun. My negative self-talk led to poor choices, including choices about how I allowed myself to be treated and ways in which I treated others. Over time, I began to grasp the true power of thought as well as my own power to control my thoughts. I realized I didn't have to let the negative Voice in My Head rant about everything that was wrong with me and with life.

I began to cultivate positive thoughts and expectations. As soon as I did, I started to see evidence to support the positives. It turns out that we see exactly what we expect to see. In fact, our thoughts determine our reality.

Our messages to others, which stem from our thoughts, tell others how we wish to be treated. I realized that I was sending people messages that suggested they treat me as inferior, as if I didn't matter. When I began to communicate new expectations, with words and boundaries, people began to treat me differently.

I learned to say no. This was huge for me. Typically, when someone asked or even implied that I should do something, I did it—whether I wanted to or not. I did not feel I had a right to say no. Although this was true in almost all my relationships, it was particularly true with my mother, Joe, and my kids. This created relationship problems. Even though I would do what was asked or implied, I often resented doing it and became angry with the other person for asking. To top it off, I allowed my feelings to be hurt if I asked someone to do something for me—not an easy thing for me to do in the first place—and that person told me no. Someone telling me no consistently triggered my old feelings of not being worthy, good enough, or a loser.

Learning to say no helped me live in ways that were more respectful of my own time. Until this point, I had been compulsively early to everything. The fear of making someone else wait for me consumed a lot of my time. Arriving 30 minutes early or more was standard. Therefore, when close family and friends would stroll in after the agreed time (knowing I had been waiting), I would react angrily. Underneath, however, I hurt because I felt as though I didn't matter to them.

When I began making my own time a priority, people close to me had some shocking reactions. Suddenly, others who were used to me waiting for them found themselves waiting for me. I remember an incident when I arrived at the appointed time. The person I was meeting expressed worry that something had been terribly wrong. I explained that everything was fine; I was just starting to respect and honor my own time. Today, being on time is a priority. But if circumstances get in the way and I am late, I don't beat myself up. If I am meeting someone who has demonstrated that he or she is prone to be late, I plan accordingly, to ensure that I'm not wasting time waiting.

Also, I had to rethink everything I had believed about forgiveness. I had always believed forgiveness was a gift you gave the person who had hurt you. I came to understand that forgiveness is a gift you give yourself when someone has hurt you. To be honest, I struggled with this; it seemed backwards. I had fallen into the common trap of feeling justified in anger and resentment because of old pain and hurts.

As time went on, forgiveness became a powerful skill (yes, I mean skill). Until this point, I could offer a running list of people who had hurt me and offer justifications for my lack of interest in forgiving them. It turns out the biggest work I needed to do with forgiveness was with myself.

I came to understand that, until I learned to forgive myself, I wasn't likely to have the peace, happiness, and connection I longed for. Even as I had blamed circumstances and others for my problems, I had blamed myself for not being good enough, not working hard enough, and making bad choices. I had catalogued nearly every mistake—big and small, real and perceived—that I had ever made. It was not easy to forgive myself. It was a process. Sometimes forgiveness is still a painful process, but forgiving was the second-best thing I ever did for myself. The first was to examine the truth behind my thoughts and beliefs.

As my 10-year journey unfolded and I experienced real change within, my outer life took dramatic turns as well. One change involved the reversal of infertility. After struggling with several years of infertility and all that went with it (including surgeries,

Chapter 2
My Journey from There to Here—How I Know This Stuff Works

medications, and a highly controlled sex life), I was told there would be no more children. With no medical answers to explain the infertility, I experienced a profound sense of loss—not only because the ability to have children had been taken from me, but because the lifelong dream of having a daughter had ended.

The loss of the ability to bear a child was devastating. Sometimes it even felt as if a death had occurred. My process of grieving was in some ways shocking. I struggled with a sense of shame that the two wonderful boys I already had didn't feel like enough for me. Then, just as I was beginning to find peace, the week of September 11, I was overjoyed to find out I was pregnant. By Christmas, Joe and I learned we were having identical twin boys. I attributed the change in my body to the change in my thinking and approach to life.

By the time Henry and Zane were born, I recognized that my marriage to Joe was over. During my hospitalization the month before the twins were born, I distinctly remember not wanting Joe to visit. I knew this was a very bad sign.

On the third morning after the babies and I were home from the hospital, I broke down and cried, confessing to my mom, "The marriage is gone." Mom hugged me and simply replied, "I know, but now isn't the time to think about that; that time will come later."

I thought Mom would be stunned by my announcement. Apparently, the marriage being over was obvious to even the most casual observer. Too much had happened between Joe and me, including bad choices on both our parts, the stress and demands of his business, and the realization that I simply was not the same person I had been when we married. In some ways, I had simply outgrown our relationship.

Over the next couple of years, Joe and I both tried, at different times, to rebuild our marriage. For me, I chose to stay because I believed the boys were better off having an intact family. I saw divorce as a selfish choice and my unhappiness as my problem. However, there came a point when our family life became so chaotic and stressed that I could see it was becoming dysfunctional. At that point, I asked Joe to move out.

Within a few short months, I realized divorce was the only responsible choice for the boys; choosing to stay married would have been irresponsible. Because I had mourned the loss of the marriage in the years leading to the end, deciding to divorce, although painful, was a huge relief. In the years that followed, despite the many challenges that divorce created, I have never regretted or felt guilty about divorce.

I vividly remember the day I called my closest friends to announce my decision to divorce. Two of them had men to whom they wanted to introduce me. My initial response was, "I am a 41-year-old mother of four boys and a Jack Russell terrier. I'm not sure I'm dating material." Both assured me I was.

Before I even separated from Joe, I had decided that, if I were ever to have another relationship, a deeper connection and shared values were essential. As it turned out, I didn't have to wait long until the opportunity for a different kind of relationship became a reality. Within a couple of months, I met Larry. Our connection was immediate. Meeting Larry was like coming to a home I had never actually been to. Our initial introduction was at lunch on a Friday. Saturday evening we had dinner.

After dinner, when Larry tried to be "inappropriate" with me, I explained I had never been promiscuous and wasn't going to start at the age of 41. He laughed and said, "You and I both know it's only a matter of time before we are married." Although the statement was startling, it rang true. In fact, at 3 a.m., as I was driving home, I called my mom to tell her I had just had dinner with my future husband.

On the surface, it wouldn't seem like a marriage between Larry and me would work. Larry had taken early retirement and lived in Naples, Florida. I lived in Pennsylvania. Larry's marriage to the mother of his two daughters had ended when the girls were 4 and 7. A ready-made family of four boys—one age 21, one age 10, and a pair of 3-year-olds—seemed absurd.

For example, one day shortly after we met, Larry and I were on the phone when Henry and Zane started fussing. I told Larry, "I have to go. *Bob the Builder* is over." Larry called a couple of hours later, wanting to know why I was building onto a house that I was planning to sell.

I asked if Larry had been drinking; why would he think I was building onto the house? He replied, "Why else would you have a builder at the house in the middle of the day?" Larry had never heard of the PBS show *Bob the Builder;* he barely knew what *Sesame Street* was. The chasm that separated our lives seemed wide.

That said, exactly 50 Saturday nights after our first dinner, we married in a family ceremony on Thanksgiving weekend. The six of us, Larry and I and the four boys, married each other. Larry's sister stood as my maid of honor and El, Larry's son-in-law, served as his best man. Larry and I made a conscious choice to get married on Thanksgiving weekend, to celebrate how thankful we were to have found one another.

Although Larry's grown daughters were happy that their dad had found someone to share his life with, I'm sure they had concerns about him marrying me and my four boys. However, the girls have never expressed anything but goodwill, and they warmly welcomed me into their family.

Larry had spent the majority of his adult life alone and had often been lonely. He was no stranger to tragedy and loss. Similarly, the boys and I had had a lot of upset and pain in the years leading up to this time. In fact, although they might not have recognized it, Zane and Henry's entire lives until this time had been influenced by painful family circumstances. For all of us, this was a fresh start.

Personally, I saw my marriage to Larry as a significant part of the journey I was on to lighten my U-Haul of issues. From the beginning, Larry and I shared the commitment to be vulnerable and accountable to one another. We found courage to share who we were, where we had come from, and who we intended to become. We left pretense behind. We recognized that even healthy couples experience conflict, and we put in the effort to communicate constructively.

Because I had grown up in a chaotic family where fighting was the norm, as an adult I had been drawn to men who avoided conflict at all costs. These men often refused even to discuss issues that made them uncomfortable. My belief had been that, if there were no conflict, there would be less chaos and no dysfunction. I was wrong. Instead, I ended up with men who tended to be passive-aggressive. My relationships with these men contained no real fighting but did contain many behind-the-scenes controlling behaviors. Issues were rarely resolved because there wasn't much communication. Although my relationships were very different from those I had grown up with, they were no less dysfunctional. My decision to marry Larry was a shift and a breath of fresh air. Larry and I communicate honestly and are not afraid of conflict. Each of us is invested in growing together as a couple and as a family.

I won't say it is always easy, but Larry and I listen to each other, validate the other's point of view, and work to resolve issues. We take responsibility for our own feelings and actions rather than blaming the other.

For the boys, I saw our new family structure as an opportunity to model a different way to be a family. Larry saw it as an opportunity to have a life he had never had and thought he never would. His once quiet, orderly life was now often chaotic and noisy, but as Larry's independent days became a distant memory, the joy of being needed and loved by so many people brought a profound level of happiness.

Within a few weeks of moving to Pittsburgh, Larry confided that he always had known he would grow to love the boys, if for no other reason that they were mine and he loved me. Nonetheless, Larry was stunned by how quickly Scott, Anso, Zane, and Henry had become "his" sons. In a very short time, Larry's love for the boys was separate and independent of his love for me. Of all the beautiful things I have experienced in life, this stands alone. I could not have asked for more.

All that said, marriage and family are work, and learning to live together was not always easy. Larry, the man who had owned the same Dyson vacuum for years, wore it out in the first year with us. He also wore out two handheld vacuums in that same year. I had spent most of my years, even when I was married, feeling like a single parent. Now I found myself married to a husband who only left the house to go to the gym for a couple of hours. Yes, suddenly, there was someone to help with the day-to-day operations, but he had opinions and preferences about how things should be done.

Larry had opinions on topics that had previously been my sole domain, such as how we managed garbage, what constituted a load of laundry, who should control the television remote, and how many times a week to have broccoli. Many things were now topics to be discussed and worked out. I wasn't always thrilled with the need to discuss so much.

It wasn't long before I had the startling realization that I was no longer the most important person in the boys' lives. The boys' new dad had power tools, understood why farting was funny, and could fix anything. He had exciting traditions, like pancakes every weekend, arm wrestling, and daily dog walks. Dad had been a boxer, earned a Black Belt in karate, and had camped. My status as primary parent was seriously challenged.

I was completely unaccustomed to having a child walk past me to ask Dad for help. The first time someone got hurt and turned down my comforting lap for Dad's, I was rattled. I felt my identity slip away.

Fortunately, because of the work I had done in my personal life, I had the skills to question my beliefs about what it meant to be a good mother. I recognized that making room for a loving and capable dad to step into the challenge of some day-to-day duties provided a positive role model for the boys. In addition, they could now have the role model of a mother who pursued her own dreams and goals outside the home. Until this point, I had felt that, if I didn't have to work outside the home for financial reasons, it would be selfish to do so.

When I accepted that Larry's move into an active-dad role was not a threat, I recognized that the marriage opened up new opportunity for me. After Henry and Zane were born, I had begun teaching and coaching part-time but had limited my work because of the demands of young children. With the new family reality, my drive to have a full-time career grew.

Larry, who had retired from a long and adventurous career, was now happy to be a stay-at-home dad. He could muster up enthusiasm for shiny new appliances and errands. After more than 25 years of being a stay-at-home mom, I could not. Larry enjoyed the daily routine of running a household, and we both agreed it was time for me to expand my horizons.

If I didn't have Larry and the boys, chances are that I would work 100 hours a week; I love my work that much. The work energizes me, and my clients inspire me. I feel privileged to have had *all* the experiences I have had throughout my entire life, including that first day of kindergarten to today. If any one thing had been different, I would have had a different outcome. I'm in too good a place to accept any other outcome.

I want the same for you. That's what this book is about. My wish for you, the reader, is that this book provides guidelines and a process for you to do the work you need to do to be happier, to be more fulfilled, and to have your heart sing.

Chapter 3

When You Change Your Thoughts, You Change Your Life

According to the National Science Foundation, the average person has up to 50,000 thoughts a day. Some experts say the number is closer to 60,000. Either way, that is a lot of internal daily dialoguing!

When I first heard that big number, I thought, "No way, I'm not smart enough to think 50,000 thoughts a day!" It turns out that I am, and you are too, since many of our thoughts are not "brandy new." When you don't count the practical thinking that gets us through our days—thinking that allows us to get up, shower, and keep on task—most of our thoughts are reruns of the thoughts we had yesterday, last week, last year, and maybe even for many yesteryears.

Estimates suggest that, for most people with an untrained mind (the vast majority of us), up to 80% of our daily internal dialogue is rooted in negative thinking or at least thinking that is less than optimal. This takes a toll on us emotionally, physically, and spiritually.

If you don't think of yourself as a negative thinker, take a few minutes to close your eyes and reflect on your thought patterns. What is the first thing you say to yourself when you wake in the morning? What do you say when you look in the mirror, look around your house, drive to work, meet with clients or colleagues, get home, spend time with family, and prepare for sleep? Do you ever think your thighs are fat, your house is out of control, or you can't believe you made the same mistake again?

Unfortunately, many people's everyday internal dialogue is skewed significantly toward the negative. The dialogue is full of judgments, criticisms (of self and others), thoughts that are rooted in the past, regrets (what ifs, could haves, should haves, and whys), and future tripping. *Future tripping* is a term that describes our bouts of worry, fuss, and energy that are wasted on problems that aren't likely to happen. A recent study at the University of Cincinnati suggests that 85% of the things we worry about never come to fruition. When they do happen, 79% of us handle the situation much better than we thought we would.

Future tripping differs significantly from planning. Planning is about being proactive and responsible for your future. Future tripping is wasted mental activity that sucks the energy right out of you, with no positive outcome. For example, planning is buying insurance even though you don't look forward to ever needing it. Future tripping is having an irregular bowel movement and jumping to the conclusion you have cancer!

Who hasn't future-tripped? One thing goes wrong and before you know it, you have catastrophized your way to your worst nightmare—only to have the whole episode turn out to be nothing. Putting ourselves through such unnecessary stress might be reason to chuckle if we did it once or twice. Unfortunately, for many of us future tripping is a way of life. The practice creates undue stress because not only is the proverbial glass only half full, but it is probably going to shatter in our hands!

You may be thinking, "Okay, I get it, but what difference does defining future tripping make? I've done it all my life, and many other people do it. There doesn't seem to be a lot I can do about it." It's important to understand future tripping because there *is* something you can do about it.

HOW IT WORKS: NEGATIVE THOUGHTS LEAD TO UNHAPPINESS

Let's start with some facts to paint a picture that shows why identifying a negative thinking pattern is important. Like it or not, the #1 indicator of happiness in life is the quality of your thoughts: that Voice in Your Head. It doesn't matter where you go in life or what you have. If the Voice inside your own head is negative, judgmental, and critical (of self, others, and circumstances), you will feel insecure, anxious, angry, and stressed. In short, you will not be happy.

Chapter 3
When You Change Your Thoughts, You Change Your Life

Many people believe they would be happy if they had more money, prestige, a better house, or a new relationship. This is faulty thinking. Typically, when unhappy people acquire such things, they still aren't happy. Don't take my word for it; look at the tabloid industry that thrives on the unhappiness and insecurities of celebrities and the ultra-wealthy.

On the other hand, have you ever known someone who didn't have much but seemed happy and content in life? That person's thoughts and feelings supported happiness even in less-than-ideal circumstances. Your thoughts and feelings determine your level of happiness.

The American Medical Association claims that stress is the basic cause of 60% of illness and disease. Stress has its roots in our *thinking*, but it affects the *body* in predictable ways. Hypertension, heart attacks, strokes, digestive disorders, headaches, fibromyalgia, weight gain, many dental problems, and a host of other health issues are attributed to stress. Stress, anxiety, and worry cause even the smartest people to make dumb choices. Living with stress can seem so normal that we don't even consciously recognize it as abnormal. We were designed to be at ease and healthy. For proof, look at the word *disease;* it means lack of ease.

That Voice in Our Heads—the one that causes us to feel stressed, critical, judgmental, anxious, worried, angry, and more—gets to rule the roost because it has been with us for as long as we can remember. We don't distinguish the Voice as a separate part of ourselves, so we have very little context to help us see how it runs our lives.

Try this fun exercise to explore the context of the Voice in Your Head: Take a moment to think about how you would explain water to Goldie the fish. In theory, the explanation seems easy enough; in actuality, explaining water to Goldie would be quite difficult because all Goldie knows is water.

Goldie may have had a few brief moments without water in her life, but chances are those moments were quite stressful. So using out-of-water experiences probably won't add much clarity for Goldie about what water really is. You might say, "Goldie, it's wet, you need it to breathe, and it's the stuff you swim in," but because Goldie has been in water her entire life, she has no context to understand your explanation.

Many of us live in the waters of stressful, negative, and painful thinking that undermines our happiness and takes a physical toll. We never stop to examine the impact of what we are thinking and saying or the *validity* of it; we simply live with it without even realizing it is there.

Several years ago, a client, Dan, confessed that, if the Voice in His Head were "embodied as a separate guy, seated next to me on a plane, I not only wouldn't sit next to him, I would take another flight." Don't rush to imagine Dan as some wild-eyed crazy person whose picture could be splashed on CNN. Dan is a personable, successful attorney with a happy marriage and a high profile in his community. Unfortunately, although Dan's experience is common, his willingness to be honest about it is not.

Here is a quick and easy exercise to drive home the point that what you think about really matters. For this, the Oak Tree/Feather Exercise, you will need a partner. Both of you will stand. Your partner will simply read the directions given in the script below. You will stand with your eyes closed, listening, and following the prompts given in the script.

Here is the Oak Tree script for the reader:

- Take a deep breath, close your eyes, and visualize a massive oak tree.
- See that oak tree standing tall and proud, with massive roots running deep into the center of the earth.
- Now feel yourself become that oak tree.
- Feel your feet firmly planted to the ground.
- Feel how stable and strong you are as you feel and become the oak tree.
- Really visualize that oak tree in your mind's eye and feel yourself *be* that oak tree.

Chapter 3
When You Change Your Thoughts, You Change Your Life

At this point, the reader should reach out and gently push you (focused on your identity as oak tree) on the shoulder. Each partner should notice what he or she experiences. At the push, did you feel stable and rooted to the ground? Did the reader feel resistance when pushing on your shoulder? Simply take note of each experience.

Now open your eyes, take a deep breath, and shrug your shoulders or bounce up and down a few times. In other words, shake off the experience.

The reader should begin reading the following Feather script:

- Close your eyes again and take a deep breath.
- Visualize a feather floating through the air.
- See the feather floating, floating, and floating through the air—light and airy.
- You've seen a feather floating through the air before, so see one again in your mind's eye.
- Now visualize and feel yourself becoming that feather. You are floating, floating, and floating.
- Feel how light you feel, and enjoy the sensations of floating through the air. Notice how it feels to be a light feather floating through the air.
- See yourself being light and feathery.

At this point, the reader should reach out and very gently push you, in the role of feather, on the shoulder. Each party should notice what he or she experiences. Did you, as the feather, feel unstable on your feet? Or less planted in your stance than you were as an oak tree? Did the reader feel you were unstable on your feet when pushed? Simply notice each experience.

If you are like most people, there will be a remarkable difference between your stability as an oak tree and your stability as a feather. When I do this exercise with clients and in workshops, nearly everyone has strong physiological responses. I watch participants as their bodies remain planted as an oak tree or are unstable as a feather. The reaction is predictable because the mind knows very little distinction between what is real and what is held vividly in the mind's eye.

This is why your thoughts are so important to the quality of your life. If your thoughts focus on negativity, low expectations, and failure, these are exactly the realities you will experience. The things you worry and complain about will become the substance of your life.

THE DELETE DELETE™ TECHNIQUE

The good news is that you cannot only improve your thinking today, but you can *change* your established thought patterns and experience sustainable improvements in your thinking for years to come. Although the Delete Delete Technique is deceptively simple, it creates dramatic shifts in your thinking.

The technique works on two levels. First, it helps build thought awareness, which is a prerequisite to any change. Second, the technique helps you make gentle nonjudgmental corrections to your thought patterns.

HOW THE DELETE DELETE TECHNIQUE WORKS

- Think of the Delete Delete Technique as a super sharp scalpel for your thinking and speech, a tool that quickly and painlessly removes your negative thoughts.
- As soon as you recognize that you have had a negative thought or said a negative statement, simply think or say "Delete Delete" and replace the negative with a positive thought or statement.
- It does not matter where in the thought or statement you recognize the negativity. It doesn't matter if you are at the beginning, middle, or end of your thought or statement. For example, perhaps you become aware that you had

had a negative thought or statement 5 minutes ago. You simply go ahead and say or think, "Delete Delete."

- When you find that you have engaged in negative thinking or speech, never argue with it or entangle with it. Arguing only energizes the negativity.
- In addition to thinking of the Delete Delete Technique as a scalpel, think of it as being like the Delete button on your computer. When you hit Delete, the words just disappear. Your computer doesn't talk back to you about the validity of the statement, get snarky, argue with you, or second-guess you. It simply follows your command and deletes. That is what the Delete Delete Technique can do for your thinking and speech.

I suggest that you actively practice the Delete Delete Technique for the next three hours. Because the technique is designed to build awareness and bring you back to balance, you will begin to see rapid results with it during this time. To keep you on track during the three hours, use reminder notes or prompts. Diligently use the technique anytime you engage in negative thinking or speech.

As you move forward, a lot of negative thoughts and statements will get away from you, and that is okay. The Delete Delete Technique, like all the techniques in this book, is designed for progress, not perfection. When your negative thinking or speech gets away from you, do not criticize or judge, simply think or say, "Delete Delete."

I recently had a client who reported that she was shocked at hearing, echoing in her head, much of what her mother had said when the client was growing up. Initially, when the client started using the Delete Delete Technique, she was tempted to chastise herself, but she soon recognized that chastising herself would defeat the purpose. The idea is to build awareness and make a correction, not to build awareness and beat yourself up about it!

Here are some examples, from my own work and that of clients, that reflect the power of this technique in the context of common themes.

When I first started doing my own thought-awareness work, I recognized that I often made the statement, "I am never going to get this done." I made this statement when faced with a long to-do list, such as when working on a big project, planning for holidays, or even while performing routine responsibilities. Because I was the mother of a family of busy boys, had responsibilities for extended-family members, and was active in my community and with several nonprofits, I was giving myself the "I am never going to get this done" message almost daily. I kept telling myself I wasn't going to meet my responsibilities.

When I evaluated this thinking, I realized that the statement was almost never true; I am a responsible person who typically fulfills her commitments. During those rare times that I do not, there are valid reasons I fall short. I recognized that the negative self-talk about not getting my work done and meeting my responsibilities really stressed me out and often put me in a bad mood. I would share the bad mood with family members and be inclined to make poor choices. For example, because I was stressing out about my to-do list, I might make the poor choice to drive too fast in an effort to rush.

After I became aware of this negative thought pattern, I began using the Delete Delete Technique as soon as I recognized myself thinking or saying something about not meeting my goals or responsibilities. I would simply say, "Delete Delete; I will get this done" or "Delete Delete; I am doing my best."

As I used the technique, my thoughts began to shift. My stress, anxiety, and worry about to-do lists and responsibilities immediately began to diminish. I noticed that my driving improved as I slowed down and my thinking became present.

The most impactful insight I received because of using the Delete Delete Technique was completely unexpected. I had always seen myself as a positive person, and most people who knew me saw me as positive. However, when I started becoming aware of my thinking, I was embarrassed by how much negative thinking and self-doubt I actually engaged in! So much of my thinking and doubt had been under the radar.

Chapter 3
When You Change Your Thoughts, You Change Your Life

I have been using the Delete Delete Technique for almost 20 years. Although I still find myself occasionally future tripping about my to-do list and engaging in other negative thinking and self-doubt, I enjoy the immediate benefits this powerful technique provides.

Ruth, a client, provides another example of the power of the Delete Delete Technique. When she came to work with me, Ruth was struggling with starting her days in a frenzy of worry about getting her daughter to school and herself to work on time. Ruth confided that the thought, "We are going to be late" was the first thought she had as she opened her eyes each morning.

During the three hours from wake-up to work, Ruth guessed she thought about being late or made some statement about being late dozens of times. Her daughter, who was in kindergarten, was also in the habit of fussing about being late for school. Ruth could see that the fussing was a learned behavior her daughter had picked up from Ruth.

When I started working with Ruth in January, the school year was already half over. I asked Ruth, "How many times have you and your daughter been late to your destinations?"

She definitively replied, "We have never been late, not once." My next question to Ruth was, "Are the statements that you consistently think and say about being late even true?"

Ruth paused for a moment and replied, "No, I guess not."

I then asked Ruth if these habitual thoughts about being late made her feel empowered, happy, and responsible.

She quickly replied, "No, they totally stress me out and put me in a bad mood every day, but I can't help myself."

Ruth learned the Delete Delete Technique during our first session. By the time she returned, the following week, Ruth had a completely new perspective in the mornings and was sharing the bounty with her daughter.

Ruth reported that, when she recognized thinking or speech about being late, she would say or think, "Delete Delete; I will be on time." Because the Delete Delete Technique helped her gain awareness of her thinking, she was able to recognize other areas in her life in which negative and untrue statements were undermining her happiness, peace, and sense of well-being. Ruth was pleased that a general shift in her thinking had occurred quickly. She reported that the impact was "amazing and fun."

Gina came to see me because her lack of confidence was so bad she stayed in an unhappy relationship because she didn't think she could find a better boyfriend. She worked in a job that was significantly below her ability and educational level because she lacked the confidence to apply for anything better.

Although Gina had always been bright, she had had trouble learning in school, grown up in a harsh family environment, and often felt isolated. She reported that, even though she had done very well in college, Gina often thought or said she was stupid. Despite being good at her job and having a boss who loved Gina's work, Gina hyper-focused on any little mistake she made and felt bad about herself.

Although some people who struggle with confidence can appear quite confident and even arrogant, Gina was someone who wore her lack of confidence on her sleeve. She walked with her head down, sat hunched over, talked softly, and avoided eye contact. In short, it didn't take a rocket scientist to pick Gina out of a crowd as someone who struggled with confidence.

I taught Gina the Delete Delete Technique during our first session. When she returned, the next week, it was obvious, even before we left the waiting room, that she had experienced a shift. Gina stood a little taller, smiled, and found it easier to look me in the eye. She reported that the Delete Delete Technique was transformational.

For Gina, laying the groundwork with the Delete Delete Technique enabled her to make big changes in her life as she moved through her work with me and beyond. When she found herself thinking or saying things like, "I am so stupid; I can't believe I did that," she replaced the statement with more positive and accurate ones such as, "I did very well in college. I am smart, and I can do this." When Gina began to berate herself for a mistake, she would say, "I am doing the best I can. I made just one small mistake."

It's Time for Action

If you are like Ruth, Gina, many others, and me, you've gotten into the habit of negative thinking. Chances are you are thwarting your own efforts and sending inaccurate messages about yourself to yourself and others. The good news is that the Delete Delete Technique can help you make a quick and powerful shift in your thinking. This shift will affect your whole life.

You get roughly 50,000 chances a day to shift to more positive and accurate thinking. It's easier than you think.

Start now!

Chapter 4

Everyone Self-Soothes—Your Self-Soothing Doesn't Have to Hurt

Imagine you are having a day from hell. The battery in your car goes dead, your boss informs you he needs the latest assignment fast-tracked on his desk before noon tomorrow, and your kids are on your last nerve. What is your vice of choice to get you through the stress? Do you stuff your face with junk food, drink chardonnay, smoke cigarettes, shop, or surf the Web for celebrity gossip? Each of these actions is an attempt to self-soothe. Think of your chosen vice as your coping strategy when things get rough.

We all self-soothe. It is an innate human need to try to make ourselves feel better when experiencing stress, anxiety, frustration, sadness, or any number of uncomfortable feelings. In addition to self-soothing in times of major stress, many of us engage in self-soothing during transitions, even seemingly ordinary transitions, such as preparing for the kids to come home from school. For working parents, the period when we are coming home from work and getting ready to tackle the domestic front can be a stressful transition.

Self-soothing is an important life skill. We need to self-soothe when we are babies and throughout our lives. Babies suck their thumbs or snuggle a favorite blanket when they need to soothe themselves. However, many of us turn to negative self-soothing habits as we grow older. For some, the negative habit may have started when you were very young, when your parents gave you food in an effort to get you to stop crying. Maybe they bribed you with treats to make you feel better when you were unhappy. As an adult, you may now be conditioned to use food as the fallback to stuff down your emotions. When the going gets rough, you might habitually turn to drinking too much, smoking, nail biting, or distracting yourself with technology.

What began as a positive human skill, self-soothing, often turns into self-sabotaging behavior. The evidence shows up when your bathroom scale shows excess pounds, when you regret what you said or did when drinking, when you find yourself outside smoking in the freezing rain, when your fingers hurt from nail biting, or when you lose hours by surfing the Web. All of these are consequences of destructive self-soothing. You may not even be aware that you are stressed, hurting, or anxious, because you have become so good at masking those feelings with your negative self-soothing habits.

The good news is that you can learn to self-soothe in positive and productive ways. You can productively relieve stress and anxiety, face your fears, overcome frustrations, and feel better, regardless of your circumstances.

My personal vice has always been Coca-Cola, over ice in my plastic mug, when possible. As a kid, the symptoms of my undiagnosed epilepsy included feeling very hot at the back of my neck. I had tunnel vision and sometimes "fainted." These episodes lasted a few minutes. Afterward I would be shaky, thirsty, and exhausted. My parents often gave me Coca-Cola, and it always helped with the aftermath of a seizure. The combination of caffeine and sugar was powerful. In our house, Coca-Cola was considered to have medicinal properties for things such as stomachaches, Mom's migraines, and everything short of a cold. You had hot tea for colds!

In addition, Coca-Cola was a family treat when we watched movies or had celebrations. I grew up linking Coca-Cola with family gatherings, relief, comfort, and love. As an adult, in the first few minutes of my mom and I being together, one of us would ask, "Do you want a Coke?" Over the years, Coke became powerfully linked to soothing almost anything that ailed me. When I had the resources to stockpile as much Coke as I wanted, cold Coke was never far away. Obviously, when I was stressed, upset, overly tired, or feeling under the weather, a Coke was my vice of choice.

Chapter 4
Everyone Self-Soothes—Your Self-Soothing Doesn't Have to Hurt

I reached a point at which I could easily consume up to six Cokes a day if my stress levels were high enough or if I was struggling with pain or anxiety. A fight with my husband, kids getting on my nerves, or feelings of being overwhelmed with the demands of my day, and I would be popping tabs every couple of hours. It seems strange now, but grabbing a Coke was an automatic stress response for me. I used Coke as a soother when I felt just about any uncomfortable feeling.

When I began working to become aware of my thoughts and habits, I became aware that my Coca-Cola habit was linked with soothing my emotions as well as treating nearly all physical ailments. I recognized how detrimental the habit was to my health and my waistline! More important, I recognized that I was giving away my power to an external force beyond my control. What would happen if I ran out of Coke?

I had even spent time worrying that the company might decide to change the famous Coke formula again. That had been a nightmare in the 1980s.

My awareness grew until I realized my reliance on Coke had to stop. Using the techniques in this chapter, I not only became more aware of how my vice was negatively affecting me, I gained the tools to change my relationship with Coca-Cola and take back the control it had over my life. Today I still consume an occasional Coca-Cola. For example, when my mom and I get together, we sometimes share a Coke. On long hot days, I think of Coke, just as some guys link a hot day, grass mowing, and beer. Still, Coke is no longer my go-to vice for what ails me. The techniques described in this chapter are more effective as well as healthier for me (and you!).

Meditation is a powerful and healthy way to self-soothe. The meditation technique you will learn in this chapter is a dual-purpose technique. It starts as a simple meditation and quickly builds to the On-Demand Relaxation Technique, which is designed to help you relax your body, mind, and energy in minutes. With practice, you will learn to drop down to the meditative level easily, receive all the benefits, and return in an efficient yet powerful way.

If your idea of meditation conjures up images of hippies sitting crossed-legged on the floor in their Birkenstocks, munching on trail mix, know that meditation has gone mainstream. Meditation is now found in classrooms, boardrooms, hospitals, and on athletic teams around the world and for good reason. Meditation changes the brain. You don't have to believe me; science proves it. I'm only the messenger.

Neuroscientist Sara Lazar gave an informative TEDx Talk, "How Meditation Can Reshape Your Brain." Dr. Lazar discussed her breakthrough research. She used MRI technology to scan the brains of people before they learned to meditate. She scanned them again eight weeks later, after they had engaged in daily meditation practices.

Neuroplasticity refers to the brain's ability to change structure when you consistently engage in a behavior (such as meditation). Dr. Lazar and other researchers have found that, when you meditate consistently—for as little as eight weeks—the neurons in your brain can literally begin to communicate to one another differently.

These changes can lead to increases in the gray matter of the prefrontal cortex. This is the area of the brain responsible for working memory, executive decision making, perspective taking, and increased emotional regulation. (Think of emotional regulation as the ability to exercise some control over stress, anxiety, worry, and anger.) In addition, meditation changes the amygdala, the area of the brain associated with the fight-or-flight response to stress.

Dr. Daniel Amen, pre-eminent psychiatrist and brain researcher, has studied more than 83,000 brain scans. Many believe him to be one of the most important mental health experts of our time. In many of his talks, books, and articles, Dr. Amen discusses how meditation changes the brain. The latest brain research indicates that mediation may slow or even prevent natural age-related decline in the brain. In my opinion, meditation, like healthy eating, is something everyone should be doing.

The Simple Meditation Technique described in this chapter is user friendly and formulaic. You can learn it quickly. After you do, you can easily drop down to the meditative level and enjoy all the benefits: deep relaxation, increased awareness, focus, memory, empathy, and intuition. This meditation creates muscle memory, allowing you to use prompts to return to a meditative state quickly. Because of muscle memory, the more you practice the meditation, the more quickly your body will respond to the prompts.

When your mind wanders in the process, simply bring it back to your breathing and resume where you left off or wherever feels right. You cannot get this exercise wrong, and there are no negative side effects.

Remember, the goal is always progress and never perfection. As long as you are able to relax a little more each time you meditate or get more relaxed than you were before, you are doing great!

This meditation will take approximately 20 minutes. If it takes a little more, that is totally okay, as long the meditation fits into your time constraints. I have outlined the meditation in the section that follows.

> If you wish to listen and follow along with the meditation, it is available for download by following these steps:
>
> 1. Visit http://www.coachmonique.com.
> 2. Click the "I Bought the Book, now I need the Simple 20 Minute Mediation Technique Download."
> 3. Enter the password Iamrelaxed (capital *I*, no spaces).

THE SIMPLE MEDITATION TECHNIQUE

1. Begin by sitting comfortably. I do not recommend lying down to meditate until you become practiced with the technique. Otherwise, you are likely to fall asleep before you have finished. Initially, it is important to learn how to drop into the meditative state and come out of it in a formulaic way.

2. Take a deep relaxing breath. Close your eyes and *feel* your body in its position.

3. Be aware of your feet. For example, if your feet are flat on the floor, feel them make contact.
4. Experience the bend in your knees.
5. Feel the back of your legs, buttocks, and back being supported.
6. Be aware of your shoulders.
7. Feel your arms stemming out from your shoulders, your hands stemming out from your arms, and your fingers stemming out from your hands. If you are able, feel your energy extend out from your fingertips.
8. Bring your attention back up to your shoulders, and feel your neck resting on your shoulders. Feel your head resting on your neck, and be aware of your scalp covering your head.
9. Take a deep relaxing breath and feel the breath come in and then go out. Keep your attention on your breath as it comes in and goes out, until you feel the rhythm of your breath become smooth.
10. Take a deep relaxing breath and gently shift your attention to your toes. Quietly say to yourself:
    - I am relaxing my toes.
    - My toes are relaxing.
    - My toes are relaxed.
11. Take a deep relaxing breath and gently bring your attention to your feet. Quietly say to yourself:
    - I am relaxing my feet.
    - My feet are relaxing.
    - My feet are relaxed.

12. Take a deep relaxing breath and bring your attention up to your legs. Quietly say to yourself:
    - I am relaxing my legs.
    - My legs are relaxing.
    - My legs are relaxed.
13. Take your attention up to your buttocks. Quietly say to yourself:
    - I am relaxing my buttocks.
    - My buttocks are relaxing.
    - My buttocks are relaxed.
14. Take your attention up to your back. Quietly say to yourself:
    - I am relaxing my back.
    - My back is relaxing.
    - My back is relaxed.
15. Take your attention up to your shoulders. Quietly say to yourself:
    - I am relaxing my shoulders.
    - My shoulders are relaxing.
    - My shoulders are relaxed.
16. Extend your attention out to your hands. Quietly say to yourself:
    - I am relaxing my hands.
    - My hands are relaxing.
    - My hands are relaxed.
17. Extend your attention out to your arms. Quietly say to yourself:
    - I am relaxing my arms.
    - My arms are relaxing.
    - My arms are relaxed.

18. Extend your attention out to your fingers. Quietly say to yourself:
    - I am relaxing my fingers.
    - My fingers are relaxing.
    - My fingers are relaxed.
19. Return your attention up to your shoulders. Quietly say to yourself:
    - I am relaxing my shoulders.
    - My shoulders are relaxing.
    - My shoulders are relaxed.
20. Now drop your attention down to your abdomen. Quietly say to yourself:
    - I am relaxing my abdomen.
    - My abdomen is relaxing.
    - My abdomen is relaxed.
21. Bring your attention up to your chest and the area around your heart. Quietly say to yourself:
    - I am relaxing my chest and the area around my heart.
    - My chest and the area around my heart are relaxing.
    - My chest and the area around my heart are relaxed.
22. Return your attention to your shoulders. Again quietly think to yourself:
    - I am relaxing my shoulders.
    - My shoulders are relaxing.
    - My shoulders are relaxed.
23. Now bring your attention up to your neck and throat. Quietly say to yourself:
    - I am relaxing my neck and throat.
    - My neck and throat are relaxing.
    - My neck and throat are relaxed.

24. Bring your attention up to your head. Quietly say to yourself:
    - I am relaxing my head.
    - My head is relaxing.
    - My head is relaxed.
25. Now bring your attention to your face: your chin, cheeks, nose, and mouth. Quietly say to yourself:
    - I am relaxing my face, including my chin, cheeks, nose, and mouth.
    - My face—my chin, cheeks, nose, and mouth—are relaxing.
    - My face—my chin, cheeks, nose, and mouth—are relaxed.
26. Now take a deep relaxing breath and bring your attention to your mouth: your lips, teeth, tongue, and gums. Quietly say to yourself:
    - I am relaxing my lips, teeth, tongue, and gums.
    - My lips, teeth, tongue, and gums are relaxing.
    - My lips, teeth, tongue, and gums are relaxed.
27. Now take a deep relaxing breath and focus on your entire body. Quietly say to yourself:
    - I am relaxing my entire body.
    - My entire body is relaxing.
    - My entire body is relaxed.
28. Now take a deep relaxing breath and gently focus on your mind. Quietly say to yourself:
    - I am relaxing my mind.
    - My mind is relaxing.
    - My mind is relaxed.

29. Now gently envision the energy field surrounding your body. Quietly say to yourself:
    - I am relaxing my energy.
    - My energy is relaxing.
    - My energy is relaxed.
30. Now gently focus on your body, mind, and energy. Quietly say to yourself:
    - I am relaxing my body, mind, and energy.
    - My body, mind, and energy are relaxing.
    - My body, mind, and energy are relaxed.
31. Now take a deep relaxing breath and begin to count backwards from 10 to 1. After each number pair, feel yourself relax and go deeper. Say
    - 10–9   I feel myself relaxing.
    - 8–7   I feel myself going deeper and relaxing more.
    - 6–5   I feel myself relaxing more and more.
    - 4–3   I feel myself relaxing more and going deeper.
    - 2–1   I feel deeply relaxed.
32. Now bring your attention to the base of your spine, at your tailbone, and visualize a brilliant golden cord connected there. This golden cord is filled with positivity and a warm golden light. Each time you inhale, you draw that warm golden light and positivity up through your body, up your spinal column, to the top of your head. Then you relax and go deeper. (It can be helpful to envision your spine as a straw. Each time you breathe in, the warm golden light filled with positivity travels up through your spine to the top of your head. You relax and drop deeper into the meditative state.)
33. Now take a few moments to experience and enjoy this state of deep relaxation.

34. To return from the meditative state, take a deep relaxing breath and begin to count from 1 to 10. At intervals, become more aware but maintain your relaxed state. Say
    - 1–2   I feel myself coming out slowly.
    - 3–4   I feel myself becoming more aware but continuing to relax.
    - 5–6   I feel myself continuing to relax but becoming even more aware.
    - 7–8   I notice how I am becoming even more aware.
    - 9   I am relaxed and becoming even more aware.
    - 10   I am refreshed, relaxed, and aware.

Practice the Simple Meditation Technique twice a day, preferably in the morning and then either at midday or in the evening. Avoid practicing the Simple Meditation Technique at night when you are in bed. To maintain the integrity of this meditation, it is important that you learn to drop in and come out in a rhythmic way. If you consistently practice at bedtime, you may fall asleep and miss opportunities to come out of the meditation naturally.

If possible, take time to practice the Simple Meditation Technique at midday. Many of us experience an afternoon drop in energy. For this reason, some countries have siesta. Rather than moving to one of those countries, I usually engage in a midday meditation at my desk. The 20-minute Simple Meditation Technique can be restorative and energizing—better than a 2-hour nap. This meditation is a great investment in time.

THE ON-DEMAND RELAXATION TECHNIQUE

Now that you have learned the Simple Meditation Technique, you will use the same principles to build to the On-Demand Relaxation Technique. In the Simple Meditation Technique, you learned to relax the body one part or group of parts at a time. With the On-Demand Relaxation Technique, you will group the body into larger segments each time you practice. For example, the first time, you can start with toes and feet. The next time you can begin with toes, feet, and legs. Eventually you will be able to relax the entire body at one time.

The Simple Meditation Technique is done in the quiet, with eyes closed and the goal of deep relaxation. In contrast, the On-Demand Relaxation Technique is designed to give you access to relaxation while you are active and have your eyes open. You continue your regular activities without interruption.

To become proficient in the On-Demand Relaxation Technique, go through the prompts of the Simple Meditation Technique, beginning with the toes and working your way up through the body, *while you are engaged in the activities of your day.* The goal is to build muscle memory, to be able to use prompts to relax anytime, anywhere, and under any conditions.

After you have practiced the prompts a few times, breaking the body down into small parts, begin to "chunk" the body into bigger parts. For example, start with toes and feet. Then go to even bigger parts: toes, feet, and legs; and then toes, feet, legs, and buttocks. With practice, you will be able to relax your entire being by using the following prompts:

- I am relaxing my body; my body is relaxing; my body is relaxed.
- I am relaxing my body and my mind; my body and mind are relaxing; my body and mind are relaxed.
- I am relaxing my body, mind, and energy; my body, mind, and energy are relaxing; my body, mind, and energy are relaxed.

Within a week, with consistent practice, you will be able to relax your body, mind, and energy in under a minute. By consistent practice, I mean doing the prompts 6 to 10 times a day or more.

To manage this, link the relaxation exercise to activities you do throughout your day. For example, use the prompts each time you use the phone, get into your car, sit down, or sit at your computer. This exercise is meant to be used while you are moving through your life. Condition yourself to relax when you are sitting talking to someone, doing the dishes, watching TV, or hanging out with your kids. The dividends will pay exponentially.

On-Demand Technique in Action

A client, Greta, suffered from terrible headaches and reported feeling uptight most of the time. Her husband teased her, saying that she probably was so thin because she burned so many calories by tensing her muscles.

Greta couldn't even remember a time when she had felt relaxed. To help her ease tension, Greta generally had a glass or two of wine in the evening. She didn't see herself as having a drinking problem, but Greta did recognize just how much she depended on that wine every night. During our first session, I introduced the Simple Meditation Technique to Greta and explained how the On-Demand Technique could give her access to relaxation. She was skeptical. Although motivated and willing to try, she didn't hold out much hope. Greta reported that she had tried meditation years ago. Her mind had wandered so much that her attempts to meditate made her feel even more anxious and tense.

Shortly after we started the Simple Meditation Technique, Greta visibly relaxed. By the time we were halfway through, she was at a deep meditative level. When Greta came back to full consciousness at the end of the meditation, she was smiling ear to ear. She was blown away by how easy relaxation through the Simple Meditation Technique had been. Not only did Greta not remember a time in her life when she had been so relaxed, but she suddenly became aware of just how normalized her tension had become.

Anything can become normalized if it goes on for long enough. Greta recognized that tension had been her normal. The sense of relaxation that came with the Simple Meditation Technique had been extreme, and she wanted more of it. At the end of the session, Greta committed to practicing her meditation twice a day and consistently practicing her On-Demand Relaxation Technique throughout her days.

When Greta returned the following week, she proudly reported that the week had been a success. She was already at the place where she could experience a reliable 50% decrease in her tension and a big jump in her ability to self-soothe using the On-Demand Relaxation Technique. Greta also reported that, although she had had wine twice with dinner that week, she had for the most part been able to replace her wine habit with meditation. She felt better because of it.

It's Time for Action

Learn the Simple Meditation Technique and commit to using it twice a day. Practice your On-Demand Relaxation Technique so that it becomes a reliable way to self-soothe and feel better. Your bathroom scale will thank you, you can stay out of the freezing rain, and you'll gain more hours in your day by stepping away from the Web.

Note to self—Relax!

Chapter 5

You Have Power to Shift Your Body, Mind, and Energy To a Better Place Whenever You Need To

Take a deep breath, close your eyes, and reflect on a negative, but not horrible, time or experience. Notice how and where in your body you feel the experience. Common ways of experiencing negativity include tension in the shoulders or jaw, tightness in the stomach, and the sensation of a dark knot in the chest. There is no right or wrong way to experience a negative or positive feeling. Whatever image or feeling you get is the right one for you. When you have a clear understanding of how you hold negativity, take a few deep breaths, shrug your shoulders, and shake off the feeling.

Know that I will never leave you with negativity. So take another deep breath and bring to mind your best experience in life. It might be when you fell in love, achieved your biggest accomplishment, or enjoyed your happiest day. On the other hand, you might call to mind a positive image—for example, the face of a beloved child, a garden, or a beach. Take the time to focus on the experience or image. Then notice how and where you experience this positive reflection in your body. Common ways of experiencing positive feelings include a sense of lightness or openness, feelings of butterflies, and a sense of a pink glow. A client once reported a sensation of her "whole body smiling." There is no right or wrong way to feel a positive experience. This exercise simply provides you with insights about how your body is affected by your negative and positive thinking and imagery.

Many people have low body awareness or don't even give much thought to their body, at least until there is a judgment that something is wrong in the body, such as pain, discomfort, or something that causes disapproval when we look in a mirror. For most people—except when experiencing extreme emotions like anger, joy, or excitement—the connection between what they are feeling and how those feelings are affecting their bodies gets very little recognition.

As you continue to practice the On-Demand Relaxation Technique from the previous chapter, you will begin to build body awareness. You will become more mindful of how your body is affected by your thoughts and emotions. This is because, as you focus on relaxing a particular part of your body, you suddenly become aware of any tension that you are holding in that area. The tension may have gone unnoticed if you did not direct your attention there.

How Emotions, Body, and Memory Connect

If you are like most people, when you recall vivid memories, your body has a response similar to the one it had when it experienced the event originally. If you recall positive, beautiful memories, you feel much better than when you recall painful ones. Unfortunately, most of us get into the habit of reliving and energizing the old negative and painful stuff. We leave the positive memories to gather dust in the corner, long forgotten or rarely visited. In the process, we hurt our bodies and our moods.

Your body makes very little distinction between what goes on in real time and what you vividly recall in your mind's eye. Don't take my word for it. Here is an exercise that will help you experience it firsthand. Read the steps in the exercise through once. Then close your eyes and conjure up the images as instructed.

Imagine a large bowl of fresh lemons on a table. Focus on getting a clear image of those lemons. Now reach your hand out and pick up a lemon. Feel it in the palm of your hand; feel your fingers wrapped around the lemon. Give the lemon a squeeze and feel the skin and the dimples or ridges. Feel the firmness of the lemon.

Now visualize a sharp knife lying next to the bowl. Know that, although this knife is sharp, it cannot hurt you. Reach out, pick up the knife, and cut the lemon in half. Put the knife down; pick up one-half of your lemon in each hand, and feel the juice drip in your hands. Now bring both halves up to your nose and deeply inhale the sharp smell of the lemon. Now bring the two lemon halves to your lips and take a big suck on the juice. Feel the juice pass over your lips and onto your tongue.

When I lead a group through this exercise, I always smile as I see a roomful of students scrunching up their faces as they "taste" their lemons. Most of them experience a physiological response to the lemons—to their smell and taste. Most even experience an increase in saliva. People respond physically to the lemon because the mind makes little distinction between what is actually happening and what is being held vividly in the mind's eye.

The lemon exercise demonstrates that what you think about and vividly remember really matters. It matters because your body responds to your thoughts. We live out our thoughts in our bodies, moods, and perspectives.

Remember what you learned in the previous chapter: Because of neuroplasticity, the brain changes in response to experience. The more often we reflect and experience old negative or painful thoughts and experiences, the stronger the negative connection in our brains and bodies becomes.

For an analogy, think of a vinyl record and how the needle can get stuck in a groove. In the same way, you can inadvertently strengthen the "grooves" in your brain for negativity. This can lead to unhealthy stress, defeatism, sadness, guilt, depression, shame, and victimization. We dwell in these grooves and then wonder why we don't have the energy to be happy.

Many of us inadvertently undermine our own confidence and ability to accomplish our goals without knowing it. When some clients share just how consumed they are with self-doubt, criticism, fear, and regret, I wonder how they get out of bed in the morning. I have nothing but respect for a person who shares such feelings; I am often impressed by how well they are doing under such a heavy burden.

YOU CAN MAKE A POSITIVE CHANGE: THE INNER-SMILE TECHNIQUE

In the face of all this negativity, I have outstanding news! You can harness the full power of your best life experience to work to your advantage—anytime, anywhere, and under any conditions. The Inner-Smile Technique gives you the ability to shift your emotions to a better place.

The Inner-Smile Technique allows you to create positive new neural pathways. These become available to you under any circumstances, with a simple squeezing of the first two fingers and thumb of your nondominant hand. If you are right-handed, you will use the first two fingers and thumb on your left hand and vice versa.

This technique is designed to cue the neural pathways to fire each time you bring your two fingers and thumb together. The technique is programmed on two levels: Level 1 occurs at the conscious level, and Level 2 occurs at the meditative level.

Take a moment to recall your very best experience in life. As I mentioned earlier, this can be a time when you achieved a great accomplishment, fell in love, or felt a connection with God or nature. The experience itself doesn't matter, only that it was your "peak experience." For some people it will be their happiest time, and for others it will be an image or a time when they experienced feelings of bliss and peace.

For example, a client, Jake, had the lifelong dream of running the Boston Marathon. He had tried unsuccessfully in four separate qualifying races, each time missing his needed time by mere seconds. Because Jake was not getting any younger, he felt compelled to train hard and make qualifying for the coveted Boston Marathon a top priority. He trained hard for months and made the commitment to qualify by running in the Indianapolis Monumental Marathon.

Jake's very best moment in life came as a surprise when he crossed the finish line in Indianapolis. Jake immediately looked up at the clock to check his time, only to discover he not only had qualified for the Boston Marathon, but he had done so with 6 seconds to spare. That moment was more important to Jake than actually running the Boston Marathon, which he did the following year. The Inner-Smile Technique allowed Jake to harness the power, energy, and emotions of that peak experience. They will be available to him whenever he needs them.

After you identify your peak experience, recall as many details as you can, using as many of your physical senses as you can. Write down the memories as you recall them. Pay particular attention to the feelings you associate with this special time and where you experience them in your body. Answer the following questions:

- How did the experience feel in your body? Where in your body did you feel it?
- What do you see when you think back to that time?
- What sounds do you associate with that time: music, voices, sounds in nature?
- What touches are associated with that time: clothing against your skin, the weight of a baby in your arms, sweat on your body, etc.?
- What tastes, if any, are associated with that time?
- What smells, if any, are associated with that time?

When Jake discussed the moment that he realized he had finally qualified for the Boston Marathon, he reported specific details. Jake remembered that, even though his body was completely fatigued, he felt weightless. He felt his shorts and shirt sticking to his body and sweat dripping into his eyes. Jake tasted the salt from his sweat as he opened his mouth in disbelief at his own time. In addition, Jake heard two of his friends call his name. Watching Jake relay the story of his accomplishment told me all I needed to know: This was his peak experience.

After you have written everything you can remember about your experience and feel that you have a complete picture, it is time to begin programming your access to that experience by personalizing the Inner-Smile Technique.

Level 1: Recall

1. Making sure you are in a comfortable position, take a deep relaxing breath, close your eyes, and use your On-Demand Relaxation Technique to relax your body completely. When you are relaxed, begin to think back to your peak experience.

2. Get a vivid picture of yourself back at this special time. Now begin to recall what you felt. Allow yourself to experience those feelings in your body.

3. With the feelings firmly established, recall what you saw during that time. Make the visuals as large, bright, and bold as you can. Blow them up in your mind's eye to the size of a very large poster or even a movie screen, if possible.

4. Recall any sounds that you associate with that time. Turn up the volume on those sounds so you hear them very clearly. Make them "surround sound" if possible.

5. Now move on to your sense of touch. Make sure to exaggerate the feelings of any touches you recall.

6. When the feelings are firmly established, move on to tastes and smells, again exaggerating them to bring them even more alive.

7. Pay careful attention to the feelings associated with this time and where and how you feel them in your body. Magnify these feelings. For example, if you felt tingling, turn up the intensity of the tingling.

8. Once you have all your senses as engaged as possible and your feelings are at their peak, firmly press together the first two fingers and thumb of your non-dominant hand. Keep that pose for a full minute or longer as you relive that special time.

9. Repeat this process four times to program it into your consciousness.

10. After you have programmed the experience into your consciousness, it is time to program your Inner-Smile technique at the meditative level.

Level 2: Programming Your Inner-Smile Technique at the Meditative Level

Take your Inner-Smile memory to the meditative level by doing the Simple Meditation Technique you learned in Chapter 4.

Here are the basic steps for programming your inner smile at the meditative level.

1. Recall your Inner-Smile memory.

2. Go through the Simple Meditation Technique as outlined in Chapter 4.

3. When you are at your relaxed level, recall the magnified memory and feelings.

4. Repeat the process of putting the first two fingers and thumb together while recalling the memory, as described in the previous section.

5. Repeat this process several times.

> For your convenience, an audio version of the Inner-Smile Technique at the Meditative Level is available for download by following these steps:
>
> 1. Visit http://www.coachmonique.com.
>
> 2. Click the "I Bought the Book, now I need the Inner-Simile Technique Download."
>
> 3. Enter the password Iamsmiling (capital *I*, no spaces).
>
> 4. For optimal results, read over the Inner-Smile Technique (described in the previous section) before listening to the audio version.

Important Notes About Your Inner-Smile Technique

The idea of programming your Inner-Smile Technique is to make your peak experience come to mind automatically, so you don't have to recall it consciously each time. For best results, be consistent with the peak experience you access with this technique. If you use more than one experience, you will scatter the energy involved, by having to stop to decide which one to use at any given time.

Positive thinking beats negative thinking any day of the week, but the Inner-Smile Technique is much more than positive thinking. While using the Inner-Smile Technique, you are engaging the emotions and feelings associated with your special experience. Since like attracts like, as you spend more time focused on the positive feelings associated with your peak experience, it will become easier to have more positive thoughts and feelings. You'll see a ripple effect from practicing this technique.

CHAPTER 5
YOU HAVE POWER TO SHIFT YOUR BODY, MIND, AND ENERGY TO A BETTER PLACE WHENEVER YOU NEED TO

HOW THOUGHTS, ENERGY, AND INTUITION CONNECT

Your thoughts and emotions strongly affect your body and your reality. They influence what happens in your life. I tell my clients to begin to see themselves as magnetic and pay attention to the correlation between how they are feeling and what happens in their lives.

To get a better sense of this, recall a time when you were in a downward spiral in life. This would be a time when it didn't seem to matter what you did; things just kept getting worse or at least staying bad.

Now recall a time when you were really in the flow of life and everything was just coming together for you. Coincidences worked in your favor, the people you needed were available, parking opened up, and your favorite song came on the radio. You know what I'm talking about here. Without a whole lot of effort on your part, things got worse or better, depending on the state you were in.

Whether consciously aware of it or not, we sense the emotion or energy in our environments, particularly when they are extreme. For example, we have all had the experience of walking into a room and immediately knowing there were bad feelings between those in the room. We just knew something was off, even if everyone was smiling or acting normally. This is because we pick up the subtle or not-so-subtle energy of the room or people or argument.

Years ago, while out touring houses with our realtor, I noticed a beautiful home on a street I really liked. I ask the realtor about it. She replied, "You don't want to look at that house; that is the 'divorce house.' The last four couples who bought that house ended up divorced." When I probed, the realtor reported, "The house just doesn't have a good feel."

As you become more adept at the techniques in this book, begin to pay attention to any intuitive feelings you experience. When you are relaxed in your body, mind, and energy, your intuition will become more available to you.

My Personal Peak Experience

About a year into my coaching and training career, I occasionally still struggled with my confidence. Internal struggles sometimes made me question my abilities to provide meaningful, high quality, and relevant services to my students and clients. To top it off, I wasn't making a lot of money, so I had doubts about whether I could be financially successful. I would sometimes find the Voice in My Head repeating, "Who do you think you are, thinking you can do this work? Besides, you can't make money doing this."

On the first night of one four-week series, I asked participants to introduce themselves and say something about themselves. Of the eight people in the class, one was a distinguished looking middle-aged man. When it was his turn to introduce himself, he told the class he was a psychologist! I nearly ran from the room, screaming that my car was on fire and I wouldn't be back.

Every old self-doubt come flooding back, and my confidence melted into a puddle right there on the floor. In my mind, I was sure Mr. Psychologist was there to discredit me. I immediately became self-conscious, but I was stuck. These people had paid good money for the workshop, so I forged ahead. You had better believe I kept an eye on Mr. Psychologist and tried very hard to read his body language. I was looking for clues that he didn't approve.

Toward the end of the two-hour class, I asked if anyone had any questions. Mr. Psychologist raised his hand. I was panicked, certain he was going to ask a question I couldn't answer. Maybe he was about to play a cruel prank.

Instead, Mr. Psychologist explained that he did not have a question; he just wanted to say that, even though he was a psychologist, he felt this class had been a great continuing-education experience for him, that I had provided a lot of great information, and that he was looking forward to the next three sessions! To say I was so excited I almost peed my pants is an understatement.

In one statement, one lone psychologist validated my work in a way that was beyond measure for me at that point in my career. You can guess what peak experience I used in my Inner-Smile Technique for a very long time. A few years ago, I got a new one, but that is a different story.

It's Time to Take Action

Consistency and practice are important in successfully using the Inner-Smile Technique. The Inner-Smile Technique is not a head game; it's a neurological programming exercise. To lock your peak experience neurologically, you need to invest time. Your best experience in life is always available. It is in your fingertips—literally. Don't waste it!

Chapter 6

The Story You Tell Yourself Is Just a Story—
Make It a Good One!

Typically, children don't begin developing the ability for abstract reasoning until age 12. This means that, before your logical mind even developed, you had begun to interpret the world in ways that might still be affecting your life negatively. If you are like most people, during your childhood years you accepted as facts the beliefs and life interpretations of your parents and others. Again, if you are like most people, it never occurred to you to question these "facts."

The human mind is like a powerful computer, juggling concepts, filtering information, and constantly creating stories to explain experiences. Because everyone is unique, each of us has a different perspective about most things. Think of it as if everyone is wearing a highly customized set of eyeglasses that filters his or her interpretation of every experience in life. This explains why two people can witness the same event and report it very differently. The two people might also have opposite responses. One person may report that an event was pleasant and fun while another reports the same event as uncomfortable and scary.

These discrepancies happen between people largely because we make judgments about things without recognizing we are basing judgments on "facts" that are simply opinions or perspectives. We associate every experience with prior similar ones and have preconceived ideas of what we expect to have happen. In many cases, we are committed to the facts we believe only because someone we trusted told us they were facts before we were old enough to judge for ourselves.

For example, it is common for parents to transfer their fears to their children so that the children become fearful of things they have never experienced themselves. This is called transference. I learned from my dad and grandfather to be afraid of snakes. I had never touched a snake or even been close to one, but because my big, strong dad was fearful, it made sense to me to be fearful. I believed snakes to be aggressive, slimy, and rough to the touch.

Years into adulthood, my older son, Scott, called me out on my fear of snakes. In response, I did the unthinkable: I touched a snake. In that one touch, my beliefs about snakes over the past 20+ years were shattered. The snake I touched was actually timid, as most snakes are, and as smooth and dry as luxurious silk. Although I still don't understand the desire to keep a snake as a pet, I have fond memories of my experience with a snake so many years ago.

Sometimes the "stories" we believe are relatively harmless. Living in the suburbs, I was in no great danger from snakes, right? But other times the beliefs we have and the stories we tell ourselves can make us miserable; hold us back from fully living our lives; and wreak havoc on our goals, dreams, and peace of mind. What's worse is that we live our lives largely unaware that we have created or unconsciously agreed to these stories.

Here are some examples from my clients of stories entrenched as beliefs:

- Life is hard.
- People like us don't get what we want in life. (This statement typically arises in certain kinds of families—for example, working-class or rural families.)
- I don't matter.
- I am unlovable.
- To have money is evil.
- I'm not smart enough to be successful.
- A son is more valuable than a daughter is.

- My parents didn't love me.
- You have to have a college education to make money.

The clients who reported these "facts" are nice, high-functioning, and hardworking people. Clients who believed these statements are not whiners or complainers. In fact, most of the people who had these beliefs didn't even recognize they had them until we worked together.

Two very different former clients had the underlying belief that "People like us don't get what we want in life." Each knew he or she had family members who said and believed this statement, but both felt he or she had escaped this particular family message. As we worked together, using the Peel-Away-the-Story Technique, both found it unsettling that their lives had indeed been dramatically affected by these beliefs.

Facts and beliefs are tricky things. What makes a fact a fact? I say there are actually very few facts in the world. Yes, gravity is a fact, and we need air to breathe. These are facts. But is it a fact that you need money to live? Do you need to be smart to be successful? I've known some successful people who were not necessarily the sharpest knives in the drawer.

The difference here is not just semantics. When we believe something is true and we have an emotional investment in believing it, we filter out or disregard any information that indicates the belief is not true. When we believe something is not true, we tend to filter out or disregard any information that might prove it is true.

The Peel-Away-the-Story Technique: Five Questions That Can Change Your Life

Helen was a client who wanted to start her own business, lose weight, and increase her energy. She had no medical problems and was highly motivated, but Helen's goals always seemed elusive to her. After a couple of sessions, Helen came to the realization that she was fearful of what would happen if she were successful in her goals, but she didn't yet know why. We set out to find the underlying cause of her issue by using the Peel-Away-the-Story Technique.

After some discussion, we agreed to examine the belief behind her statement "I am afraid of what will happen if I achieve my goals." Here are the five simple questions I asked Helen about this statement:

1. Is your belief true?
2. Do you have any doubt that your belief is true?
3. Do others share your belief?
4. How do you feel when you have this belief?
5. How would your life be affected if you did not have this belief? (For this question, I generally ask my clients to think as if I could use a high-powered scalpel and remove their ability to have just this one thought.)

Helen reported that she had no doubt that she was afraid of what would happen if she achieved her goals. She knew that her husband did not have any fears about what would happen if Helen achieved her goals, so her answer to the third question was no.

When asked about her feelings surrounding this belief, Helen reported that she felt scared, powerless, depressed, angry, and hopeless. I asked how Helen treated herself when she thought of this belief. Helen reported eating junk food, like pizza or french fries. If these foods weren't available, Helen turned to candy or other sweets. If junk food wasn't available and Helen was not engaged in an activity at the time, she might begin using her smartphone.

When I asked Helen how her life would be affected if she did not have this belief, she responded that she would be free, happy, and relieved.

Then I asked Helen to close her eyes and visualize herself as if she had achieved her goals of starting her own business, weighing less, and increasing energy and activity in her life. What would she look like?

She responded, "I would be more visible, and that is scary."

In the face of this belief (a deeper one), we started over with the questions, using the belief "Being more visible is scary."

When I asked Helen if being more visible was scary, she reported that yes, it was scary.

When asked if she was sure it was scary, she reported that, even though she didn't know why, yes—it was scary.

When I asked Helen if everyone shared her belief that being more visible was scary, she conceded by saying, "No, lots of people probably enjoy being visible."

Then I asked Helen how she feels when she thinks the thought, "Being more visible is scary." She reported that, although her reaction seemed silly, she felt anxious when she had the thought. It made her palms sweat.

Then I asked Helen how her life would be affected if she were not capable of having the thought "Being more visible is scary."

She reported it would be freeing, so I asked Helen to close her eyes, visualize herself being more visible in her life, and imagine what that would be like.

She responded, "My parents would see me."

At this point, both Helen and I knew we were on to something. The realization was obviously painful for her, but Helen wanted to continue and explore the question.

Now we had an even deeper belief to question. I asked, "Is it true your parents would see you?"

Helen responded, "Yes."

I asked her if she was sure this was true. She responded, "Yes."

When I asked if everyone would agree her belief was true, she said, "No, people would say my parents see me now."

I asked her how she felt when she had the thought, "My parents would see me." She answered, "Scared, upset, and ashamed."

When I asked Helen how her life would be different if she could no longer have the thought "My parents would see me," she responded with "free, alive, and courageous."

Then Helen had an epiphany. When she was a kid, she had always tried to hide from her parents, particularly her mother. Helen's mother often gave Helen various messages that told her to go away or stay out of the way.

Helen recalled how her dad would come home from work each night with a bag of takeout food for her. He would give her a kiss and a hug, asking her briefly how she was. Helen then took her bag of food to the game room in the basement. She ate it in front of the TV, alone. When Helen grew to be a teenager, she would take the food to her room. Throughout all her years growing up, except for holidays and special occasions, Helen's parents sat together in the kitchen, talking and eating food that Helen's mom had made for them while Helen ate takeout alone in another part of the house. Helen recalled also that, until she was 13, the family car was a big station wagon. Even though she was an only child, Helen's parents always encouraged her to sit in the very back.

Helen talked about how she and her mother were never close and that her mother was always very critical of everything Helen did. Helen's dad was less openly critical, but he was a perfectionist who had very high standards for Helen in nearly every area, including her behavior and grammar.

For Helen, the questions in the Peel-Away-the-Story Technique brought everything together. As a kid, she was consistently encouraged to stay away from her parents. The message was clear: Go eat in another part of the house and sit as far from us as possible in the car. When Helen was around, her mother would tell her to go away, and criticize even minor details of her life. Helen's dad had such high standards that Helen consistently worried about disappointing him.

Helen understood that being seen was necessary to business success. The Peel-Away-the-Story Technique helped her understand that, because she had such a fear of being seen, she kept herself overweight and dressed "dumpy" in an attempt to make herself invisible. Because Helen had gotten both overt and subversive messages that being seen was not good, she had organized her life to remain unseen. She worked in a nondescript office in a cubicle where she didn't have to relate with many people. She arranged her life and that of her family (husband and baby) so that as a threesome they were largely self-contained. The family didn't participate in many activities outside immediate family and home.

Helen's "glasses" were highly customized to filter out opportunities that would make her more visible. She typically dealt with the loneliness of isolation by turning to food, just as she had done with the takeout her dad used to bring.

Helen had developed her root belief, "It isn't good to be seen," when she was very young. However, like most of us, she had forgotten that she had simply accepted the belief as true. When Helen had goals that worked in opposition to this deep underlying belief, she would sabotage herself with food, isolation, and procrastination.

How the Peel-Away-the-Story Technique Works

The Peel-Away-the-Story Technique serves two functions. The first is to take a thought or belief that holds you back and discover the underlying belief. If you aren't sure what thought or belief to start with, get in a relaxed state, using the On-Demand Relaxation Technique, and ask yourself about a goal you have that you have been unable to accomplish. Relax and just let it come up. Address whatever comes up, using the questions in the Peel-Away-the-Story Technique to help you discover what is holding you back.

When your goals are in direct conflict with your strong beliefs, it will be nearly impossible to accomplish your goals. If you do accomplish them, you will most likely sabotage yourself in some way so that you still lose out in the end. For example, think of how many people quickly divest themselves of money when they get it. From lottery winners to weekly-paycheck earners, many people have issues around getting, having, and keeping money. This leads them to lose whatever money they get.

People who believe that they are unlovable provide another example. Such people find it difficult to find someone who loves them. If they do find a partner or mate, the likelihood of their maintaining the relationship is low.

Without realizing it, we undermine ourselves and then wonder why success, security, love, and happiness are so elusive. The Peel-Away-the-Story Technique is a powerful way to uncover the deeply held beliefs that cause you to self-sabotage.

The Peel-Away-the-Story Technique's second function is to increase your awareness as you move through your days. Listen to the Voice in Your Head and the way you speak. These reveal patterns of belief that may or may not be true.

Notice when you use words such as *should, have to,* and *can't*.

I tell clients, "Don't 'should' on yourself." When you find yourself using self-sabotaging language, quickly go through the five questions of the technique and examine your answers. When there is no significant emotional charge, you can often find truths quickly. For example, when you say you "have" to do something, you may realize that the behavior you have to do used to be important to you but is now just a habit. Peel-Away-the-Story is a great technique for cleaning up big and little issues in life.

For me, the day my beloved denim duster was stuffed into the toilet in junior high, I decided (accepted the belief) I was a loser who couldn't have nice things. Years later, I could vividly recall the humiliation I felt that day, standing there seeing my duster in the toilet. The loss for me was profound and so painful it could still bring me to tears decades later. Not only was the duster a luxury (it had cost $100 at a time my family lived on $200 a week), but my dad, with whom I did not have a very good relationship, had taken me to a swanky store to buy it. The value of that duster could never be measured in dollars.

Without realizing it, from that day forward and for years to come, I became someone who longed for material goods to prove I was not a loser. When I was a teenager, I worked at McDonald's. After I covered my expenses and bought gifts, I spent all my money on clothes and accessories. Later as an adult, I craved nice things, often putting myself in debt to have them.

My drive to prove myself other than a loser created problems in my marriage to Joe. Up until a few years ago, I would not leave the house, even to go to the bus stop to pick up my kids, unless my hair, make-up, and clothes were perfect. I wouldn't keep anyone waiting, but you can know for damn sure I arranged my day to look my best. Although I still enjoy nice things and the privilege of being able to look nice, my positive self-image is not tied to looking perfect.

I had to peel away the story many times and dig deep, but eventually I was able to recognize that I wasn't a loser growing up. I had simply believed the message that I was a loser. In fact, considering the obstacles I had to overcome, I had done better than could ever have been expected. I was many things, but I was not lazy either. That was another false message I had believed.

Most days now, I enjoy hard-won self-love and acceptance. I have the confidence to do things I previously had only dreamed of doing—for example, writing this book. Writing a book is a bold move because a book is out there in print forever for your critics to see and judge.

It's Time to Take Action

Have you ever examined the thoughts and beliefs you adopted as facts before you had even developed a logical mind? If not, these beliefs may be negatively affecting your life. These beliefs may be blocking your path forward.

When you feel passionately about accomplishing something and are motivated but find yourself blocked or unable to meet success, use the Peel-Away-the-Story Technique. If the problem is a repressed or long-standing belief, the process may take a while, but it will be worth it.

Chapter 7

Feelings and Intention Attract—
Make Your Focus Positive

What you think about really matters. Unfortunately, most of us focus our thoughts and attention on what is "wrong," what needs to change, and what makes us unhappy. Then we wonder why we keep getting more of the same and why getting new and improved things and experiences is so hard.

Gregg Braden is a former computer systems expert with Martin Marietta Defense Systems and Cisco Systems and the author of *New York Times* best sellers about ancient wisdoms. Braden tells us, "Our mentality becomes our reality so it makes sense that by changing our mentality, we can change our reality." In other words, when we turn our thinking around and imbue it with positive emotional energy, we dramatically increase our chances of getting the changes we want. We attract what we think about. We have the ability to create conscious intentions that attract what we want.

You may be familiar with the movie *The Secret*, which involves setting positive intentions, and say, "Oh, I saw that and tried setting intentions, but it didn't work for me." Although I think Rhonda Byrne did a good job of introducing the idea of creating intentions, the movie has a drawback. It focuses too much on materialism. There is nothing wrong with material goods and even luxury, but these things will not bring you happiness. I can personally attest to this. I believe that *The Secret* leaves out a very important aspect of creating intentions: underlying beliefs. If we want to attract happiness, luxury, and positive relationships, positive thinking is not enough. We have to believe we deserve these things. That belief is an inside job. It doesn't matter how much you think positively about having that perfect relationship if deep down what you think and believe is "Who would want to be with me? I'm overweight and boring." You are going to continue to want the relationship for a long time, but you are not likely to actually get it.

To repeat, getting and keeping positive real change is strictly an inside job, so focusing on external things in the hope or belief that you will finally be happy is faulty thinking. Unless you correct the underlying belief, if you do get the things you desire, you will experience a heart-crushing blow because you still won't be happy. You will have to face being wrong all along. If you remember, that is what got me started on the path to this work nearly 20 years ago.

THE SCIENCE BEHIND INTENTION

The human brain has a high-speed powerful "program" called the reticular activating system. Your reticular activating system filters all the information available to it and highlights the information that is pertinent or in agreement with what you are focused on. Your reticular activating system minimizes the information it sends that does not fit well or align with what you believe or expect to see and experience. For example, when you are hungry, you see food. When you are unhappy, you see things to confirm your unhappiness: loneliness, fear, others seeming to have so much more, etc.

Here is an experiment to drive home the point. I recently read, in *AutoWeek Magazine*, that only 2% of cars on the road in the United States are green. I'm guessing that, unless you have a green car, you would agree that there are very few green cars on the road. We can then agree that we are not likely to see many green cars when we are out.

Over the next week, I want you to be aware of green cars. Think about seeing green cars and expect to see them. Then watch what happens. Once seeing a green car becomes important to you, you will see them regularly. That is because your reticular activating system is now filtering for green cars! The same thing happens when you begin looking at and test-driving a certain kind of car. You suddenly see them everywhere. This is the power of focus.

Chapter 7
Feelings and Intention Attract—Make Your Focus Positive

Once green cars have meaning to you, you see them. This shift in your experience occurred even though you aren't emotionally invested in green cars. Imagine what can happen when you invest emotion as well as intention in your focus.

As we move forward, you will learn not just to shift your attention and focus, but to energize it with emotions so that you can more easily get and achieve the things that are important to you.

Get Ready for the Setting-an-Intention Technique: Keep These Rules in Mind

As you use the Setting-an-Intention Technique, remember these points:

- Thoughts, feelings, and language all dramatically affect your reality.
- Your brain has a powerful system in place to recognize and attract (good or bad) what you need to become aware of to fulfill your expectations, beliefs, and goals. Remember how we demonstrated this with the example of green cars.

Until this point, you may have been using your thoughts, feelings, language, and brain to work against you. Fortunately, today is a new day.

Every day your brain generates thousands of thoughts. You have myriad emotions and infinite experiences. Now is the time to learn to organize and infuse your thoughts and emotions with passion and focus, to help you get what you want. In the Setting-an-Intention Technique, you will use your reticular activating system and the power of your thoughts and emotions to help you see and recognize opportunity, possibility, resources, and connections. These will lead you to experience what is necessary for you to get what you want out of life.

For intentions to work, you must follow some ground rules. First, you must believe it is possible for you to have what you want. If you don't believe it is possible, you are dramatically less likely to get what you want. If you do get it—whether it is health, wealth, a home, a relationship, or anything else—you will not be able to hang onto it.

You can test your beliefs by doing your meditation while focusing on your beliefs about what you want. Examine any thoughts or feelings that come up. If you get thoughts or feelings that are in direct opposition to your goals, use the Peel-Away-the-Story Technique to discover your underlying false belief or fear.

The second rule for setting intentions is to use the technique for things that are significant or important to you. If you can't conjure up some passion and focus, your energy will scatter, and this will greatly diminish your chance of success.

The third rule is to use one intention at a time. Having too many intentions means you will partially focus on a number of intentions but fully focus on none. This will undermine your efforts.

The fourth rule is vitally important: When doing the Setting-an-Intention Technique, focus on the three to five characteristics that are the *result* of what you want. Do not set intentions about *how* you get there.

When you set intentions about how you think you must achieve your intention, you cut off infinite possibilities regarding how you may get what you want. For example, if you set an intention to get a better job, allow that job to come to you however it is meant to. It may come as a promotion at the company where you currently work. It may come as a job at another company, or it may come as an opportunity in the form of a business venture. You stack the deck in your favor when you accept the outcome without strings attached. Don't worry, the result will come to you as a good thing, even if it doesn't necessarily feel that way initially.

THE SETTING-AN-INTENTION TECHNIQUE

1. Think about a specific area of your life in which you feel passionate about making changes. For example, do you want a meaningful relationship, a new

career, or a different home? It doesn't matter what change you want; it only matters that the change is important to you.

2. After you have decided on what you are going to use your Setting-an-Intention Technique, choose three characteristics that define what it will feel like to have your intention fulfilled. For example, if your intention is for a new career, what will that career look and feel like? Invest time in getting a feel for the level of excitement and energy of that career. Even envision what it will physically look and feel like.

Here are some questions you might ask, getting a clearer and clearer picture with each answer:

- Will you be sitting at a desk or standing in front of people, making presentations?
- Will you be working at home in your pajamas or dressed to the nines in a suit?
- Will your new career have a casual feel or will you be energized by the positive stress and fast pace?

Whatever characteristics you choose, notice how the characteristics affect your body and how and where you feel the excitement physically. So, if you are going to be spending a lot of time sitting at a desk, see and feel your body in the chair and leaning into the desk. If you are going to be standing and presenting, feel yourself standing at the front of the room and looking out to your audience.

Three to five characteristics is the ideal range because this number paints a picture for you and allows you to key in to your emotions and senses, without diluting your energy and focus.

Remember, think and feel about the characteristics as if you already have them. For example, when you open your closet to get dressed in the morning, *visualize* and *think* about getting dressed for that new career. When you drive to work, *visualize*, and *think* about what it feels like to be driving to such a great career. As you drive home, *think* about how rewarding your day was in your new career. Focus on your intention in the morning when you get up, and as you go to bed at night.

Stop thinking about what needs to change, and focus on what it is you want to have as if you already have it. You have already focused and felt the unhappiness with the current condition. Now it's time to shift your focus and emotion to better things. This can be a sticking point for some people because they initially feel as if the exercise takes them out of touch with reality. Think about it this way: You have been generating stories and negative feelings that had absolutely no basis in reality for years. Don't discriminate now that doing that can help you!

Take note here: You will still need to attend to your current responsibilities so don't tell your current boss, "I won't be available for the meeting tomorrow because I have another job," unless the new job is already a reality. I don't want you calling me asking for a job because your boss just fired you! Instead, each time you think about work, *think*, *feel*, and *experience* in your body how exciting or good it feels to have the new career. Remember: You attract that on which you focus, good or bad.

3. Get yourself an *intention mirror,* the bigger the better. By this, I mean get an ordinary mirror to help you do extraordinary things. Many people use poster board or wall space as an intention board. I always insist on a mirror because, each time you look at the mirror, you actually project yourself into the story of what you want in your life. I tell clients to consider keeping the intention mirror (or the entire intention exercise) a private project unless you have people in your life who will be supportive. If, for example, you have a spouse who is going to tease you or make fun of your intention or intention mirror, his or her

Chapter 7
Feelings and Intention Attract—Make Your Focus Positive

input may undermine your confidence. You decide if keeping the project private is right for you.

4. Place your intention mirror in an area that you frequently either enter or pass through. Then look at yourself in your intention mirror as often as possible. For example, if you use your bathroom mirror as your intention mirror (assuming you live alone or have let your significant other in on your project), each time you look in the mirror *visualize, feel,* and *experience* how good life is now that you have what you desire.

   Here's how you develop your intention mirror: As you shift your attention and energize your feelings regarding your intention, you will begin to notice things that remind you of or represent your intentions. Examples include pictures in magazines or images on the computer that "speak" to you. You might notice words in print or advertisements of people who currently do or provide support services for what you intend to do. Objects that represent your intention may catch your attention. For example, a necktie or scarf that would be appropriate for your new career might really speak to you. Collect all such things. Once a day, spend about 10 or more minutes placing your images, objects, words, etc., onto the mirror. Do this work while *visualizing, feeling,* and *experiencing* your complete intention as if it is already a foregone conclusion. Stay focused and deliberate; make the activity almost ceremonial for yourself. Allow your intention mirror to be a work in progress, adding things each day and making changes to the mirror to accommodate new expressions of your intention.

5. When looking into the mirror, really allow yourself to get excited about it. Do you remember what you learned when visualizing an imaginary oak tree and feather in Chapter 3? You learned that our bodies make very little distinction about what is going on in real time and what is held in the mind's eye. By using

your intention mirror with emotion and excitement, you are increasing the "juice" of your intention.

6. As you go through your day, each time you think about the Setting-an-Intention Technique, *visualize*, *feel*, and *experience* yourself as if your desire has already come to pass.

7. Finally, each time you *visualize*, *feel*, and *experience* yourself experiencing your intention, express gratitude that you have what you want. Gratitude is a very strong emotion with the power to transform lives, so use it with your Setting-an-Intention Technique.

What If You Are Not Successful in Your Intention

If you follow the steps for setting an intention and are not seeing the results you expected, carefully consider the following questions:

- ❑ Are you putting forth the right kind of effort? For example, if your goal is to meet a new life partner, you must actively engage in activities or choices that align with this intention. You can't sit home and expect the perfect person to ring your doorbell.

- ❑ Are you being realistic? For example, I can set an intention to be a great singer, but I simply do not have the voice to pull it off. My intentions must align with my abilities.

- ❑ Is your intention too narrowly defined? For example, if your intention is to have a peaceful family, and you define peaceful as having zero conflict, your intention will not become a reality.

- ❑ Is your intention in conflict with your beliefs? For example, if you have a deeply-held belief that you don't deserve the job for which you set an intention, you probably won't get (or definitely won't keep) the job. If what you desire is in opposition to a belief that you hold, your belief is likely to win over the desire.

If you find yourself struggling with your intention work, I suggest rereading Chapter 5 and completing the Peel-Away-the-Story-Technique.

INTENTIONS WORK! CASE STUDIES

MONIQUE

Several years ago, when I decided to move from a home office into full-time office space, I set an intention for my ideal office. The characteristics I defined for my office were

- Pleasant, enjoyable environment
- Flexible space that accommodates both one-on-one coaching and group training
- Conveniently located
- Plenty of parking
- Having a sense of community

I had been talking to my friend, Dan, about renting space in a new 30,000-square-foot facility that he and his partners were building. The space would eventually house his salon, spa, and event-media business. Dan and I have similar values and a similar work ethic. We support one another's businesses; Dan sends me clients and does my hair, and we collaborate on some projects. It seemed so likely that I would rent from Dan in the new facility that I had even started doing some work at his current location.

However, I stayed focused on my Setting-an-Intention Technique, visualizing and feeling myself in the ideal location. Several weeks before I expected to finalize the rental deal with Dan, one of Dan's partners, Rohn, informed me of a change. Because of some reconfiguring of the new space, he was unsure if there would be room for me. He would let me know within a few days.

I was surprised, but I stayed focused on my intention and took comfort in believing that the intention would come to pass. The following week, Rohn informed me that there would be no room for me at the new location. He was sorry. I remember hanging up the phone, disappointed, but confident the intention would work out somehow.

The next day, Rohn called me back to say that, because of the new facility, he would be moving out of his current office, which happened to be 500 yards from the new location. He gave me the contact information of his property owner, Bill. Rohn assured me that the office he was moving from was a great space. When I checked out the office the next day, I discovered it met each one of the characteristics I had laid out. Not only that, the space was very nicely furnished and I found Bill, a professional polygraph specialist who also works in the space, to be an interesting person.

I find the science of polygraph fascinating enough that I have read a few books on the subject. Now, when there is a break in my schedule, I have interesting conversations with Bill and some of the other people in Bill's part of the space. In fact, one specialist keeps offering to hook me up to a polygraph so I can experience it, but we haven't gotten around to it yet.

Shortly after I moved into my office, I had a hair appointment with Dan at his new location. As I toured the beautiful facility, Dan confided in me that the acoustics were a problem. It turned out that, every time someone walked across the floor upstairs, it sounded as if he or she were walking on the heads of the people below. In addition, you could hear right through the walls when people were talking; Dan and his partners were going to have to do some serious insulating. Poor acoustical insulation would have been a major problem in my business, which is all about talking and sharing details of one's life. By leasing Rohn's old office, I had avoided a hassle. Dan's new space is beautifully quiet now, and I am happily ensconced in mine.

CHAPTER 7
FEELINGS AND INTENTION ATTRACT—MAKE YOUR FOCUS POSITIVE

CHRIS

My client Chris came to me because she had been single for 3 years after her 20-year marriage had ended. She lacked the confidence to "get back out there." Chris thought she wanted to find someone to spend her life with but wasn't sure what she wanted: a long-term monogamous relationship, another marriage, or someone to live with but not marry.

For a couple of weeks Chris and I worked on her confidence and the negative messages from the Voice in Her Head. She was having success making positive changes, so she and I felt she was ready to move forward with the Setting-an-Intention Technique. Chris set the following intention: I am in a loving relationship with a man who is

- ❑ Honest
- ❑ Funny
- ❑ Sexual
- ❑ Loves the water

From the very first day Chris activated her intention, she began to move through her days feeling the safety of being in an honest relationship. She would feel her face breaking out into a smile or laugh, she spent time *visualizing* and *feeling* what great sex felt like, and she visualized herself enjoying water and having fun.

Chris completed her sessions with me a few weeks later, excited and optimistic. The following week, she called to say that at a conference she had met a man, Ron, who "should have been a comedian, he was so funny." Not only did Ron have a boat, he had a pool.

Of course, it was too soon to know if he was the "one." They had just met, so Chris didn't know Ron well enough to know if he was honest. They hadn't been intimate, so Chris wasn't sure about the sex. Early indicators showed promise.

I told her I was proud and excited for her and asked her to keep me informed. Over the next few months, Chris let me know that Ron seemed very honest and willing to share his past mistakes with her. In addition, things were great in the "sex department."

When Chris and I talked a few months later, she let me know she and Ron were in a committed relationship and were spending several nights a week together. They were doing some traveling with the boat and spending time in Florida, near the water. Even so, Chris was surprised by how much she still enjoyed living alone and having time when she didn't have to "answer to anyone." When we last spoke, Chris felt that both she and her man were happy with the way things were and probably would continue to keep separate houses but spend a lot of time together doing things they both loved.

It's Time for Action

Remember the words of Gregg Braden: "Our mentality becomes our reality so it makes sense that by changing our mentality, we can change our reality." The Setting-an-Intention Technique is available to help you to harness the power of your own thoughts, passion, and energy. Don't miss the opportunity.

Begin to think of yourself as a magnet. Pay attention to what you are thinking, feeling, focusing on, and expecting. Set an intention by defining three to five characteristics that are important to you. Create an *intention mirror,* and put yourself into the new reality you are creating. Enjoy how quickly life can change.

CHAPTER 8

YOUR HEART HAS TRANSFORMATIVE POWER—
CULTIVATE HEART INTELLIGENCE TO ACCESS THAT POWER

YOUR EMOTIONS INFLUENCE the physiology of your heart. If you are feeling stressed, anxious, or fearful, for example, your heart produces a jagged, irregular rhythm. In contrast, if you are experiencing a sense of love, joy, or peace, your heart produces a smooth, harmonious rhythm. Which do you think is better for you?

Every language has words that refer to the heart as a physical organ and an emotional center. When we are happy, we use language such as this:

- My heart is full.
- I love them with all my heart.
- My heart is bursting with joy.

When sad or angry, we use language such as this:
- My heart is heavy.
- My heart is closed.
- My heart is broken.

The whole world uses language like this, and the whole world has been doing it since the dawn of language. Philosophers, poets, and even doctors use metaphoric language about the heart. There is actually a syndrome known as broken-heart syndrome, sudden heart failure that comes after emotional trauma.

EXPERIENCES OF THE HEART

Think back to a time when you were in the presence of someone who was treating you or someone else badly and you could sense the person's heart was closed or hardened. As you reflect, notice how this person's energy felt to you. How did your heart feel in response?

Now think back to a time when someone was treating you lovingly and you knew that person had only love in his or her heart for you. As you reflect, notice how the energy felt to you. How did your heart feel in response? Very different, right?

We have all had experiences of feeling the positive vibe someone puts off. It feels soft, safe, warm, or loving in that person's presence, and we want to be around him or her. In contrast, we have all had the experience of being around someone whose vibe is uncomfortable to us, someone we don't enjoy being around. The vibe around this person is angry, heavy, or dark. Your feelings in such experiences aren't in your imagination; there is science behind them.

Our hearts and brains communicate with each other. When we feel positive, uplifting emotions in our hearts, our brains get the message to decrease cortisol, the stress hormone. Our brains also get a message to increase our DHEA (an antiaging hormone) and increase our oxytocin hormone. Oxytocin is associated with intimate gestures, such as handholding, hugging, breastfeeding, and sex. When we feel positive, uplifting emotions in our hearts, our whole body chemistry is influenced positively.

The heart has an intelligence all its own. Think back to a time when you just "knew something in your heart." Too often, we intellectualize and ignore the wisdom of the heart. We go with our heads and later regret it. But heart intelligence can help us gain insight, tap into our intuition, and guide us in ways that our logical mind simply cannot. Our logical mind is linear and filters out anything incongruent with what we believe, expect, and focus on.

Given the power in our hearts, it would be foolish not to harness that power for positive change. The Heart-Centered Breathing Technique is a simple process that, within minutes, can transform your feelings (and your physiology) about negative circumstances, memories, people, situations, or places.

THE HEART-CENTERED BREATHING TECHNIQUE

1. Sit quietly and simply focus on your heart (in the center of your chest) and your breath.

    Keep your attention on your heart. If your attention wanders, simply bring the focus back. If you struggle to keep your attention focused on your heart, try placing your hand over it.

    You may notice your breath gets uneven as you begin this exercise, but breathing generally becomes smooth in three to five breaths.

2. Keep your focus on your heart and your breath, but now visualize and feel your breath flowing in through your heart. Continue until your breathing feels smooth and balanced, not forced or awkward. Again, your natural rhythm will come about in three to five breaths.

3. Now *visualize* and *feel* the breath come in through your heart and flow out through your solar plexus, which is at the top of your stomach and right under your rib cage. Do this until you feel the natural rhythm of the breath coming in and going out.

4. After the rhythm is established, gently focus on a positive feeling, such as love or gratitude, and *visualize* and *feel* yourself breathe in that feeling. You can use an image that signifies the feeling to you or simply focus on the words. For example, visualize the word love and allow yourself to feel love. Then begin to breathe love through your heart. If you are using an image, breathe that image in with feeling and let it continue through the exhale until you have a natural rhythm. You might feel as though there is a circle that extends from your body as the breath comes in and goes out.

5. If you are struggling with a negative emotion after you have completed step 4, intentionally focus on something positive on the inhale. Release the negative emotion on the exhale. Likewise, if you are struggling with a particular person or circumstance after you have completed step 4, intentionally focus on something positive about that person or circumstance. Breathe that positivity in on the inhale. As you exhale, release the negative emotion or feelings.

6. Notice the positive inward and outward changes you see and feel in yourself.

You can use the Heart-Centered Breathing Technique anytime you experience negative circumstances, memories, feelings, people, situations, or places.

- Use the Heart-Centered Breathing Technique throughout your day. The more you use it, the less you will need it.
- When you find yourself struggling with a person or circumstance, if possible, close your eyes and do the Heart-Centered Breathing Technique. If it is not possible to close your eyes, do the technique while keeping your eyes open.
- If you are near someone during a difficult interaction or if that person is struggling with pain (physical or emotional), complete the steps of the technique for yourself. Then think of the person you are with. You don't need to tell the person what you are doing. Simply *visualize* and *feel* that person's energy as you include it in your positive feelings.
- Strive for progress, not perfection. After you learn this technique, it will come very naturally. You will be able to create positive sustainable shifts quite easily.
- Try beginning and ending your day by doing the Heart-Centered Breathing Technique and focusing on one or more of these feelings: peace, love, or gratitude. These feelings affect your body and your life in powerful ways.

THE HEART-CENTERED BREATHING TECHNIQUE PRODUCES POWERFUL SHIFTS IN RELATIONSHIPS AND HEALTH

I had an ex-husband who made some very bad choices. On the surface, I was nice and tried to get along, but underneath my heart was broken—not so much for myself but for our son. Because the circumstances surrounding his dad's choices were so painful for our son, I was hurting in a way only a mother can. I wanted to take away my son's pain, but I couldn't. This made my heart ache even more. I struggled because I was angry with my ex-husband, but I knew that anger wasn't helping anyone, including our son.

I made a commitment to use the Heart-Centered Breathing Technique each time I thought of, saw, or spoke to my ex-husband. I was highly motivated, so I was consistent in my practice. At first it was hard, despite our many good years together. The last years had been very difficult, and the choices that affected our son seemed overwhelming.

As I followed through on my commitment, I noticed an almost immediate shift. As time went on, my heart softened toward my ex-husband. Now, although I wouldn't call him a friend and I am sometimes frustrated with his behavior, I am able to love and accept him. I am able to be grateful for having my ex-husband in my life. Despite the relationship's difficult ending, my ex-husband was a primary relationship in my life for many years, and that means something. I truly and honestly want him to be healthy, happy, and successful. The Heart-Centered Breathing Technique allowed me to shift from negative and stressful reactions to positive ones when dealing with this man who will be forever linked to my life. Both my body and my mood are better for the change the technique allowed. And my vibes regarding my son's father influence my son as well.

It's Time for Action

For most of us, the heart doesn't get much attention unless we are having health issues or focusing on preventing disease. Because breath is an automatic physiological response, we don't often think about breathing until we are having trouble with it. Then suddenly we recognize just how precious breath is! The fact that we can utilize our heart and our breath together to help us transform negativity to positivity is a powerful gift available to us always. Use the Heart-Centered Breathing Technique to create real and lasting change in your life.

Get to the heart of the matter. Sit quietly and shift your attention to your heart. Envision sending out positive, loving vibes and see your life begin to change.

Chapter 9

Talking and Communicating Are Different Things—Make Sure You Are Communicating

EVERYONE TALKS, BUT FEW PEOPLE COMMUNICATE really well. Communication is complicated, and it's not something you master once and for all. Throughout my whole journey of personal growth, I've been learning about communication, and I still am. Sometimes I get it right, and sometimes I still struggle. I am definitely improving. The good news is that effective communication is a skill; you can learn it. Both you and I can continue to refine our communication skills.

No one technique or formula can ensure that you communicate well in every situation, but guidelines in this chapter will increase your chances of success. We will cover the following formulas:

- ❏ Show up in productive ways.
- ❏ Follow basic communication guidelines.
- ❏ Respond to conflict constructively.
- ❏ Set healthy boundaries.
- ❏ Listen to understand.
- ❏ Learn the art of the apology.
- ❏ Guard against defensiveness.

Show Up in Productive Ways

Stephen, a 30-something IT professional, came to me as a client because the owner of his company recognized him as a high-value employee. Unfortunately, the owner was considering firing Stephen because of the problems he created in the workplace. In short, Stephen did not "work and play well with others."

When Stephen was offered coaching with me, he accepted it even though he didn't recognize his need for it. He only agreed because he wanted to keep his job!

Soon Stephen began to see how his behaviors and attitudes affected others at work. He recognized that, because he struggled with low self-confidence and a sense of not belonging, he often found reasons not to attend meetings or participate in discussions. When he did attend meetings, Stephen sat quietly and did not participate.

Stephen was stunned to learn that many of the people he worked with saw him as arrogant and felt that Stephen perceived himself to be superior to them. After all, he avoided others and rarely spoke. Saddled with low self-confidence, Stephen felt anything but superior. His coping strategies had backfired because many of his co-workers now had negative (and inaccurate) perceptions of him. Stephen realized he had suppressed the feelings surrounding his low self-confidence and focused on becoming great at the technical aspects of his job. Now he could see his technical skills weren't enough.

As we worked together, Stephen began to gain confidence and see how he could relate to others at work in positive ways. He began making it a point to attend meetings and contribute. In addition, Stephen worked to make connections with his co-workers during routine encounters.

As our work progressed, Stephen began to explore how our work together was affecting his personal life as well as his work life. Stephen expressed discomfort about his wife's busy social life—because that life didn't include him. In the past few years, Stephen's wife, Irene, had taken up numerous activities, and Stephen increasingly found himself home alone. Irene had tried to include him for years, but Stephen had typically either expressed little interest or put in little effort. Now Stephen could see where always being the "no person" had unwittingly communicated that he didn't want to be included. Irene had acted on that message.

When Stephen could make the connection between his actions and their unintended consequences, he was empowered to be accountable and begin to do things differently. Stephen chose to have a frank discussion with his wife about how he could now recognize that he had isolated himself in their marriage. He explained that he wanted to begin to do more things together. When Stephen was able to show up in a different way both at home and at work, his life began to change for the better.

Your behavior and words as you show up in a relationship determine how others treat you. If you don't like how you are being treated in any relationship or situation, examine the messages that you are sending. Are you expressing a desire to be engaged and included, or disengaged and isolated? Are you building a reputation as a "no person" or a complainer, or as one who is open, positive, and flexible?

FOLLOW BASIC COMMUNICATION GUIDELINES

Even when you show up productively in relationships, communication can be like an obstacle course.

Here is a list of basic communication guidelines that will help you overcome the most common obstacles:

- ❏ Take body language into account. Notice both your own body language and that of the other person. If you are talking and the other person is sitting with legs and arms crossed, save your breath—that person isn't receptive. If you are the one sitting with arms and legs crossed, shift your attitude and your body posture. Open both your mind and your body.
- ❏ Make eye contact and give the other person your full attention. Your full attention conveys respect, a gift. When you give a person the gift of your attention, he or she automatically softens.

- Take timing into account. Avoid jumping on someone the moment he or she walks through the door at the end of a workday. Avoid bringing up difficult topics first thing in the morning or close to bedtime. For serious discussions, choose times when both parties are rested and alert.
- Organize your thoughts. Before a complicated or difficult discussion, take the time to prepare what you want to say. Choose three well-thought-out points. If you try to communicate a large number of points in any discussion, you'll have a scattered, confusing exchange.
- Put your smartphone down! Hiding behind technology is an avoidance technique. Note to parents: Do not attempt to compete with TV or technology. Speak once and, if the kids don't give you their full attention, remove the technology. Then they'll pay attention!
- Stay focused on the current issue. Avoid bringing up old stuff when in a conflict; this just heightens the emotional charge and makes it difficult to resolve anything. Keep the current issue in focus.
- Keep things simple and clear. If you are talking about a complicated issue, break it down into smaller parts so it can be more easily understood. Speak clearly and, when possible, tell a story by giving an example. Storytelling is the oldest form of education and communication. The mind likes and grasps stories because they create pictures.

Respond to Conflict Constructively

Conflict is an inevitable part of life, especially in close relationships. In a primary relationship, a major disagreement a week is considered average and healthy.

Complete lack of conflict is a sign of a problem. The problem is most likely one of two things. Either one person suppresses his or her own needs and opinions for the other person's sake, or there is an unspoken rule that difficult topics are not discussed.

Chapter 9
Talking and Communicating Are Different Things—Make Sure You Are Communicating

You can relax: Conflict is normal, even good. Healthy conflict involves hashing things out. It's not always easy, but it helps you to build strong relationships.

As I said earlier, there are no "good" or "bad" emotions, only positive and negative reactions to emotions. So, when you have anger or other emotions that result in healthy conflict, use the emotions to create change.

Change can come in many ways—a shift in how tasks are completed, how people are treated, or how time or money is spent. Sometimes change won't be possible or won't happen on a schedule that you prefer. In those cases, agreeing to disagree can allow everyone's opinion to be heard and validated without anyone having to be "wrong."

Sometimes compromise is the appropriate way to resolve conflict, but if one person is the one who always gives in and repeatedly over compromises, this might be a sign of an imbalance of power. Chances are that the over compromiser's needs are not being met.

If you are the one always giving in, recognize that your behavior is sending a message. You are communicating that you are reliably willing to compromise or allow your needs to be secondary. To change the pattern, you need to change your message. Consider giving the other person an updated lesson on how you want to be treated in the future.

Here is a formula for effectively communicating during conflict:

- Use "I" statements. Speak for yourself rather than the other person. Do not say things like "You ignore my needs." Instead, say, "I feel as though my needs are ignored."
- State what you heard. Do not say, "You said. … "
  Instead say, "I heard. … "
- Describe what you saw. Do not say, "You did. …"
  Instead say, "I saw. … "

- ❏ Explain how you felt rather than blaming the other for your feelings. Do not say, "You made me feel. …" Instead, say, "I felt as though. … "

Be specific at each step, and avoid being judgmental. You might even set a time limit to keep things productive. Do not beat the subject to death. A good rule of thumb: Speak one sentence for each of the above.

As you communicate, avoid blaming the other person for what's wrong in the relationship. Although blaming the other may feel good, blaming renders you powerless in the end. When you blame others, you put yourself in the position of victim. Real victims are powerless. When you are powerless, you are not in a position to make changes. Blame robs you of the chance to look inside yourself and grow because of what you see and experience. Blame is not your friend. It is your enemy.

SET HEALTHY BOUNDARIES

Unfortunately, sometimes we are in situations or relationships with people who have zero interest in effective communication or even respect. The primary interest of the other person is getting his or her own way by controlling you or the situation.

Name-calling, derogatory statements, and aggression are not acceptable. Everyone has a right to feel safe, respected, and independent. If you do not feel these things in a relationship or particular circumstance, take responsibility to either leave the situation or set boundaries that align with your needs.

Setting a boundary paints a clear picture of the problem, as you see it, and lets the other person know what behaviors you will or will not tolerate. Setting a boundary is not about the other person; it's about you. Setting a boundary is not trying to control the other person; it is about controlling yourself and your experience.

Here is a formula for setting a boundary:
- ❏ State the problem as you see it.
- ❏ Give one or two concise examples of the problem behavior.

Chapter 9
Talking and Communicating Are Different Things—Make Sure You Are Communicating

- Explain how you feel when the behavior happens.
- Explain what, if the behavior continues or happens again, you are going to do to remove yourself from the situation.

There's an important distinction between a boundary and a threat. A threat is generally about how the other person is going to be punished or treated. A threat is typically intended to hurt, control, or even destroy a person or experience. A boundary is about you. A boundary states what you will do in response to specific behaviors. The other person may be affected, but he or she is not the target.

A couple of weeks ago, I was in a meeting with Barbara, a colleague. In the first hour of our meeting, both her husband and 20-year-old daughter telephoned. Barbara explained that she had told each of them she was going to be in a meeting and had instructed them not to call her unless there was an emergency. Barbara was annoyed when both her husband and daughter called to ask trivial questions. She and I had a brief discussion about boundaries, and she asked me for advice.

I suggested that Barbara set a boundary, letting both her husband and daughter know that she would no longer answer unnecessary calls when working. Here is what she decided to say to them:

- When I left for my meeting today, I asked that you not call me except in an emergency.
- During the meeting, you each called me, even though I had explained I was unavailable except for emergencies. I took each of your calls because I was afraid that something was wrong.
- I feel as though my work is disrespected when you call me with questions that can wait until I get home.
- If you call me again for a nonemergency when I am working, I will begin to turn off my phone when I am at work. I don't want to turn off my phone, in case a true emergency occurs. But if calls continue, I will feel as though

turning off the phone is my only choice. My work and professional image are too important to me to allow this to continue.

Barbara felt good about her boundary and was willing to stick to her word, if necessary. Barbara was following a very important rule: *Never ever set a boundary you are not willing to keep.*

For example, imagine you tell someone you are not going to tolerate him or her screaming at you during an argument. You state you will walk away and not return to the conversation until he or she can talk calmly.

If the screaming happens again, simply walk away calmly. Don't remind the person of the boundary. If you stay in the situation, even to remind the person of the boundary, you are teaching the other person that your word is not good and that the other person's behavior can control you. If you do not keep your boundary, you teach the other person that you do not mean what you say or say what you mean.

If you are new to setting boundaries, the process can seem futile or scary on paper, but trust me: If you stick to your boundary, the other person will continue the unwanted behavior for only a time or two. Soon the person will realize you have set up new rules for what was likely an old game. Patterns emerge in relationships very early on, so chances are the behavior you are looking to avoid now is one that has been around for a while. Chances are you sent a message you would tolerate it.

Be careful to choose boundaries that are comfortable and doable for you. To set extreme boundaries is to set no boundaries. An example of an extreme boundary is "If you do that again, I'm never going to speak to you" or "You are grounded until you go to college." Such a boundary is an empty threat because you'll never follow through. There is a big difference between empty threats and boundaries.

LISTEN TO UNDERSTAND

One of the best ways to communicate effectively is to listen with the intention of understanding and to speak with the intention of being understood. Most of us have this one backwards: We listen with the intention of responding. In the process, we miss valuable information. Admit it, when someone is talking, you are busy in your own mind, deciding what you are going to say as soon as you get the chance to say it.

Here is a list of things to strive for to increase the effectiveness of your listening:

- Wait. Give the other person your attention and wait for him or her to finish speaking before you speak. Don't interrupt.
- Paraphrase. Reflect what you heard to let the other person know you were listening and that you have the gist of what he or she is saying. This way, if you misunderstood, the correction can be made without further confusion.
- Be congruent—be sure your gestures match your words. For example, don't raise your voice in anger and smile. Pay attention to your tone and volume; make sure both are appropriate for the situation and message you are trying to convey.
- Be clear and direct. If you have something difficult to say, be clear about that from the start. Don't bait and switch, because that can lead a person to feel attacked. It can also make you appear dishonest or untrustworthy.

LEARN THE ART OF THE APOLOGY

Taking responsibility for your words and behavior is a sign of strength, not weakness. When you admit that you are wrong, people respect you. When you act defensively or refuse to admit you are wrong, you appear weak as well as unreasonable.

Here is a formula for how to apologize concisely and effectively when you have been wrong:

- Ask the other person for a moment of his or her time.

- ❏ State clearly how you were wrong. Acknowledge that you understand how your actions hurt the other person.
- ❏ Take full responsibility for your actions. Do not tie your mistake to the other's behavior or in any way signal that the other person had it coming or contributed to your mistake or choice.
- ❏ Be clear that you have learned from your mistake. Express your plan to change your behavior or do things differently in the future.
- ❏ Ask the other person to hold you accountable. Ask the person to bring your attention to the matter if you should happen to be in the wrong again.
- ❏ Say you are sorry or apologize.
- ❏ Close with a positive. Let the other person know you appreciate or love him or her. Let that person know you intend to contribute to a positive relationship.

Guard Against Defensiveness

We all have the urge to be defensive, but this simply doesn't work in our favor. Defensiveness undermines us in the eyes of the other person, even while it prevents us from making positive change.

When we are defensive, it is because on some level we suspect what the other person is saying is true. That activates a fear within us.

Generally, our fears reflect issues such as self-doubt, not being good enough, feeling inadequate, not belonging, being unlovable, shame, regret, or distrust in our ability to control our behaviors. Of course, we usually do not recognize the underlying fear. Instead we feel angry and the need to defend ourselves. Defensiveness seems like a safer, less painful route than facing what is underneath. However, facing our fear sets us free.

For example, if you know you are good at your job and someone in a bad mood makes a comment that implies that you are incompetent, it is easy to see that the comment is the other person's issue. In this instance, you are not likely to judge yourself negatively. However, if you struggle with underlying fears of inadequacy, you are likely to be defensive about the person's comment. You may have a snarly comeback or point out a fault of the other person because your fear of inadequacy has been activated. If you don't say anything to the person in response to the comment, you may feel the need to share what was said with others so that you can defend yourself as you relay the story. Even if you don't speak about the issue to others at all, you will find yourself becoming defensive to yourself.

When you feel yourself getting defensive, activate your On-Demand Relaxation Technique. This will bring your stress, anxiety, and fear levels down. When you are calm, ask yourself if there is any possibility that what the person is saying is true. Sometimes you can recognize that the other person is just lashing out because of his or her own issues, making it easier for you to let the issue go. However, often you can recognize that you have an underlying fear. You might fear that the other person is right and not want to see that part of yourself. To get clarity for yourself, take some time to use the Peel-Away-the-Story Technique to uncover the underlying belief or thought that is making you fearful.

Defensiveness can feel safe—even powerful. But in actuality defensiveness is weakness. Defensiveness blocks you from looking inside yourself and growing because of what you see. It also keeps you stuck in the chaos, pain, and struggle that go on within you when you don't address your fears.

How a Christmas Gift Transformed How I Show Up and Communicate

When I was growing up, I did not feel heard or understood much of the time. I believed no one cared what I thought or had to say. This wasn't necessarily true, but it's the story

I believed. I grew up feeling powerless and familiar with the feelings surrounding unmet needs.

As an adult, I developed a habit of repeating myself, especially during emotionally charged conflicts or times when I felt powerless or disrespected. During arguments with family members, the other person would often ask me to quit repeating myself. Even when I recognized what I was doing, I seemed unable to stop. I would think to myself, "Just one more time and this person will understand."

Many times I understood that I had valid points and reasons to express myself or even be angry, but I could not get others to hear me. Sometimes family members would use my habit of repeating to refuse to talk to me about difficult issues. Other times they let me talk while sending signals to let me know they weren't listening. Emotional discussions and arguments were rarely productive. Real change in my relationships was slow and laborious.

Then one Christmas I opened a gift from my brother and sister-in-law, Eric and Luci. It was a toolbox, carefully stocked with tools and beautifully wrapped. I had once mentioned, before Christmas, that I needed my own tools to use around the house. I was in the process of purchasing my first home and knew that tools would come in handy.

My initial reaction upon opening the gift was shock. The Voice in My Head screamed, "I was heard! I was heard." I was elated more with the gift of being heard than I was with the toolbox itself.

Gift giving is an important event in our family, so my reaction wasn't to getting a gift, even one I had asked for. I reacted because the toolbox was a highly unusual gift for me, and I had expressed my need for it only once, in passing.

I am not handy or inclined to take on projects around the house that require items stored in a garage. Although I had asked for the toolbox and tools for my new role as a homeowner, unconsciously I did not believe I would be heard or get what I desired. At some level, I believed the gift didn't fit in with how I felt people saw me: incompetent, lazy, and unmotivated.

When I opened the toolbox, I recognized that Eric and Luci had not only heard me, but validated my desire even though the desire was atypical for me. I realized also that they and others did not see me as incompetent or lazy. I realized that I had an internal fear that I was that way. That day, I began the long process of exploring the pain of my many years of feeling incompetent as I struggled through school.

I had been accused repeatedly of being lazy at school; at home, my mom had accused me of making everything hard. Growing up, I came to believe these messages. I came to believe that, because of my inadequacies, I wasn't worthy to be heard. This became the story I told myself. It became the way I showed up in relationships.

When Eric and Luci gave me the toolbox, I had an experience of being heard—an experience that created insights for me that continue to unfold today. I'm still realizing that, when I show up differently, people treat me differently.

For example, I recognized that, for many of my years of being a mother, I expected my kids (as I expected everyone else) not to listen to me. Therefore, I consistently repeated every piece of important information. Eventually I would get on their last nerve, and the kids would get an attitude with me. This behavior would activate my fear of not being heard and not being important. Things would go downhill from there. My expectation not to be heard became a reality when I consistently repeated myself. My own behavior caused the very outcome I feared.

As I pursued my personal growth, I learned the reasons I felt the way I did. I was comforted to learn I was not alone. I discovered that such understanding was not only my personal passion, but my life's professional work. All that was good news.

I began reading a lot of science and research and studying experts in the fields in which I was interested. This was mixed news for my family. I learned to reduce my incidences of repeating myself, but I developed the habit of citing statistics, research findings, and experts when I was trying to make a point. This was my new way to try to get people to listen to me.

It took a while, but I recognized this was just a different side of the same coin. On some level, I still didn't expect to be heard, taken seriously, or seen as competent. So I used science to ensure that people listened to what I had to say. I had simply gotten more sophisticated at hiding my fears.

Although all my newfound wisdom helped me to be successful in my career, it did not necessarily make me a popular lecturer at home! At first, I would get defensive and feel bad that my loved ones didn't want to hear about the science that proved the things I was saying. Eventually I saw my defensiveness for what it was: a way to bury my fears that I was incompetent and that no one would listen to me.

Today, I sometimes repeat myself but acknowledge the habit when it is brought to my attention (at least most of the time). I still fight the urge to pepper my discussions with statistics or science. Sometimes I still lose the fight. However, today I feel freer just to express myself and expect others to listen. The change has gone a long way in helping me build successful, profoundly meaningful relationships. These are my greatest gifts in life.

Although learning to communicate effectively hasn't always been easy (for me or my loved ones), the process has meant discovering, questioning, understanding, and coming to terms with my own my personal beliefs about being heard; having needs; being competent; and ultimately, the power of my own voice. The work has changed how I show up in relationships, which has changed how others treat me.

In addition, I had to learn, as we all do, the skills involved in genuinely listening to others, communicating productively in conflict, setting boundaries, and apologizing when I am wrong. I had to recognize that doing wrong or making a mistake doesn't make me a bad or dumb person.

Chapter 9
Talking and Communicating Are Different Things—Make Sure You Are Communicating

It's Time for Action

Learning to communicate well is not easy, and it's not a once-and-for-all kind of skill. It is, however, a skill well worth your investment. Good communication is the bedrock of healthy, happy relationships.

Make it a project to review the guidelines in this chapter, one group at a time. Practice the guidelines or steps in that group until they become a skill. Then move to the next group. Start with the group that will have the most impact on you and your relationships.

CHAPTER 10

BACKSLIDING IS INEVITABLE—STEP INTO THE
NEXT BEST VERSION OF YOURSELF TO KEEP FACING FORWARD

THE FAILURE RATE OF NEW YEAR'S RESOLUTIONS IS 93%. I don't need to be a math wizard to know that's a dismal outcome. I don't have to be a wizard of any kind to be certain that you've failed at any number of goals you've set. We all have.

When we fail at our goals, we feel bad about ourselves. When we feel bad about ourselves, we typically do more of the very thing we had resolved not to do, creating a negative spiral.

For example, let's say you resolve not to yell at your kids and then do exactly that (and what parent doesn't yell?). Now you are likely to yell even more because you are frustrated and angry with yourself for yelling in the first place.

Let's say you resolve to diet and lose 20 pounds and then eat cookies or go a week without losing a pound. Because you start to feel like a failure, your chances of raiding the snack food cupboard go way up. You either eat to make yourself feel better or because you think, "What the hell. I blew it, so why not have some cookies?"

Our thoughts about setting goals or changing habits are often worse than unrealistic. Our own thoughts can inadvertently undermine us before we even get started. Our first mistake is to focus on the negative or the wrong in our lives. I've placed this chapter toward the end of the book for a reason. I hope that by now you've learned the pitfalls of focusing on the negative. Here is a fundamental law, as reliable as the law of gravity: If you focus on the negative, you'll attract more of it.

A second mistake is to engage in black-and-white thinking in terms of our goals. In the process, we give ourselves a very narrow definition of success. For example, either you lose 20 pounds or you don't. If you don't lose the 20 pounds, you judge yourself a failure, resulting in poor self-image and low confidence. As a result, you return to doing things the same way you have always done them, getting more of the same outcomes and results.

We make a third mistake when we try to make changes, such as breaking a habit (overeating, smoking, overspending, or yelling at our kids) without identifying the underlying issues, thoughts, or beliefs that created the habit. Even if we are successful in achieving our goals initially, we will be unlikely to sustain the new behaviors if we don't address the core issues, thoughts, or beliefs.

In order to create sustainable change, you need to define your goals in a context that helps you achieve them. When you change your approach toward goals and use the Stepping-into-the-Next-Best-Version-of-Yourself Technique, you stack the deck in your favor because you leverage the things that you are doing well already.

When you leverage the things that are going well in your life, you'll find it easier to get more of the same. When your focus becomes the positive rather than the negative, you create the space needed to do better than you are currently doing—without being as vulnerable to failure.

In addition, as you use techniques you have already learned, such as the Peel-Away-the-Story Technique, you will gain insight into the underlying fears, beliefs, or thoughts that have been contributing to your self-defeating habits. It's what we don't know that we don't know that runs the show. Until you recognize your underlying thoughts or beliefs, you won't be able to address them, making sustainable change nearly impossible. You can't change when you are in conflict with yourself.

You may desperately want to change something in your life (for example, your job). If your underlying belief is that you don't deserve that change (a better job), you are not going to get the change. Sometimes your insights will be relatively quick and easy. Other times the process will be longer because you have to learn through repeated experience. Either way, be open to the process. Don't put too much pressure on yourself, because pressure can create unhealthy stress, which inhibits progress. As always, it is about progress, not perfection.

THE STEPPING-INTO-THE-NEXT-BEST-VERSION-OF-YOURSELF TECHNIQUE

1. Allow yourself more than one narrow definition of success.

    For example, if you define success as losing 20 pounds, anything much less than losing 20 pounds is failing, right? So broaden the definition to be more realistic and forgiving: make the goal to be healthier! This may seem like mere semantics, but it is not.

    Chances are that, unless you are on death's door, you already have some modicum of health. By setting a goal to get healthier, you focus on what you already have—what you already do right. If you need to lose 20 pounds, my guess is that you could benefit from more exercise as well as from making improvements in your diet. In addition, there may be other factors contributing to your being overweight. For example, studies are now linking lack of high-quality restorative sleep with weight gain, particularly in the midsection. Your body needs rest to have energy to function. Insufficient sleep increases your body's craving for sugar and carbohydrates. This leads to weight gain.

    In addition, if you constantly tell yourself, "It's hard to lose weight" or "I'm never going to lose weight," your own negative self-talk diminishes how you feel about yourself. This has a dramatic negative impact on your ability to choose healthy behaviors. Furthermore, if you have a history of eating to self-soothe when stressed or unhappy, that pattern, if not addressed, will keep undermining your success.

When you take a longer view and expand your definition of success, you can create a target list to help track your progress, recognize your successes, and shift your perception toward change.

2. Declare it!

Share how you plan to do better on your newly defined goals. Confide only in people who are supportive and positive about your goals and who will not berate or judge you if you experience a setback. For example, if you have a positive and loving relationship with your mother, sharing with her your plan to be more patient with your kids and not scream so much is likely to result in her support. As a mother, she understands the challenges you may face, and she loves and supports you. If you don't have a positive and loving relationship with your mother, choose to share your goal with a supportive friend instead.

When you share your goals, you build accountability as well as support. This can be helpful if you lose perspective or objectivity about yourself or your goals. When I coach clients, holding them accountable or providing a boundary for them helps them gain insight and keeps them focused on their priorities.

For example, this past winter, on a brutally cold day, Josie called to ask if she could reschedule her appointment with me. Josie and I were working together to help her make changes needed to transition into her own business.

Josie explained that her company had allowed employees the option of working from home that day because of the weather. She said, "I really don't want to get dressed and make the drive to your office."

I responded, "I am here, and I have several other clients on the schedule who are keeping their appointments. Josie, would you have gone in to work if your boss hadn't given the option of working from home?"

She answered, "Yes."

I answered, "Okay, the weather is unpleasant. But does missing your appointment with me match your priorities?"

There was a long pause. Then Josie responded, "I see your point. Although I want to start my own business, I see that I am allowing a small obstacle to deter me from moving forward. I think I do this a lot."

This exchange gave Josie an insight she needed to address an internal dynamic that was holding her back. Until that point, Josie had believed the road to success involved managing time, developing a business plan, and making contacts. Josie had not seen how she procrastinated and often felt stuck because of fear of starting her own business. She was focusing on the wrong areas for improvement. No wonder she wasn't moving forward.

3. Acknowledge your improvement.

Give yourself credit where credit is due. Don't wait for perfection before giving yourself a positive acknowledgment. Taking just 2 minutes to feel and experience the smile on your face and feelings of accomplishment in your body, mind, and energy helps you to build positive body awareness and strengthen the neural pathways for good feelings.

Remember, like attracts like, so the more good feelings you have, the easier it will be to have more. Too often, we don't take the time to stop and actually acknowledge and appreciate our successes, particularly the smaller ones. Yet small successes lead to bigger successes, so this is a vital step in your process.

4. Document your success.

Keep a running list of your successes so you can look back and appreciate them. It is human nature to forget the good and remember the bad. In fact, there is probably evolutionary significance to the fact that the bad is so much more memorable. The more attuned to bad experiences early humans were, the higher the likelihood they would be around to pass along their genes to the gene pool. For example, it is all fine and good to remember how delicious a newfound berry tasted, but it is vital to remember that the berry made you sick or, even worse, poisoned to death your next-door caveman.

When you document your successes and progress, you have a chance to re-experience positive emotions. If you are someone who naturally enjoys journaling, use a journal. If not, keep a quick and easy grocery-style list. Write your successes in bulleted-list style and keep the list handy on your desk or, better yet, by your bed. At the end of each day, list your successes for that day and reflect on previous successes. This gives you a boost right before you fall asleep.

5. Recognize that the goal is progress, not perfection.

Don't make an all-or-nothing game of your goals. That is New Year's resolution–style thinking. Although perfection may seem like a positive goal, it often turns out to be a negative one. Perfection usually requires many things to align internally and externally. Even if the alignment happens, perfection isn't sustainable because the world is forever changing.

When you shoot for perfection, you will end up feeling as if you are a failure. With progress, not perfection, you can see a setback for what it is, an isolated event. A setback is an event you can learn from rather than a black mark against yourself.

You don't have to have a perfect day to have a good day. Let's return to our example of improving your health. If your food choices weren't great at dinner, but you hit the gym, got a good night's sleep, used your Inner-Smile Technique at work instead of hitting the vending machines, and used your Delete Delete Technique to improve your self-talk, you can consider the day good. You made progress, and that is positive every time.

The Stepping-into-the-Next-Best-Version-of-Yourself Technique is likely to result in your achieving the changes that you want. More important, it will help you sustain those changes.

Yet even when we use broad definitions of success, obstacles and setbacks are inevitable. Planning for obstacles and setbacks increases your chance of success, because planning prevents you from being thrown off the track when confronted with them.

OVERCOME SIX COMMON OBSTACLES

1. Build awareness of how your world is changing.

   When life catches us off guard, we typically react rather than respond. Building awareness allows us to change this pattern. When we react we may not be aware of our choices and behaviors. Our reaction may be rooted in fear or the perception of lack or threat. The change that results from reacting may not be for the better. When we respond, we think about what is happening and choose to adjust or change in positive ways. Learning to respond rather than react will empower you and give you the conscious control to step consciously into the next best version of yourself in spite of setbacks.

2. Put your baggage down.

   As we have discussed in earlier chapters, in childhood we begin collecting our proverbial baggage because of things such as family dysfunction, profound loss, learning problems, socioeconomic issues, abuse, or significant negative experiences. Because of your baggage, you may struggle in adulthood with poor self-image, fear, control issues, the need to please, perfectionism, inability to set appropriate boundaries, or low confidence. This is the time to recognize your baggage and where it came from and then to understand that you are an adult now with far more control than you had as a child. Probably your circumstances are drastically different.

For example, if you had real and legitimate fears as a child, acknowledge that. Also understand that those same people or situations can't hurt you now unless you allow it to happen.

If the only way you received love and positive attention as a child was to be a people pleaser within your family, recognize that now you have other choices and can build different kinds of relationships.

As part of your progress, recognize that continuing to live with outdated patterns is no longer accurate, necessary, or even appropriate. Outdated patterns hold you back.

3. Build awareness of your habits, beliefs, and patterns.

   Our habits become ingrained, and we develop muscle memory of them. For example, I had a client who wanted to quit smoking. When he recognized he had the habit of lighting up a cigarette every time the phone rang, he was able to change the habit.

   Anytime you have unexamined beliefs, thoughts, emotions, or behaviors that are rooted in your baggage, sustainable change will be nearly impossible. Once you examine these things and reject those that are no longer appropriate, real change is possible. As I said earlier in this chapter and as I always tell my clients, "It's what you don't know that you don't know that runs the show."

4. Be aware of your emotions.

   If you are experiencing anxiety, fear, sadness, anger, or frustration, chances are you are extremely uncomfortable. Examining your emotions for validity can be the necessary first step to positive change. For example, if you are feeling fearful, ask yourself if there are valid reasons to feel unsafe. Or is the fear part of an old pattern that should be examined? In addition, when making changes, understand that a certain level of comfort with discomfort is necessary. There are no universally guaranteed outcomes.

Chapter 10
Backsliding Is Inevitable—Step into the Next Best Version of Yourself to Keep Facing Forward

5. Make changes in your environment to support the next best version of yourself.

    Environment plays a key role in our choices and successes. Chances are that, if you struggled to make changes in the past and were unsuccessful, your environment was one element that helped to keep you stuck in your old ways.

    Engaging in activities that play to your strengths is important. For example, choose to spend time with people who are supportive of you or who share your goals or vision for change. Use your Setting-an-Intention Technique to create a story and pictures that better align you with the changes you want to make.

6. Make friends with the Voice in Your Head.

    As you learned, the quality of your self-talk is the major indicator of success in your life. Make it a point to shift to positive thinking and self-talk. Use the Delete Delete Technique every time you become aware of thinking that undermines you, makes you feel bad, and stresses you out. As you build awareness, you will notice shifts in how you show up in your own life.

I recently had a client, James, who wanted to step into the next best version of himself to get healthier. He decided not to diet, because he wanted flexibility and he wanted to use skills he had learned by working with me as a coaching client. Because James had dramatically changed how he saw himself and had learned to positively self-soothe, he wanted to use the Stepping-into-the-Next-Best-Version-of-Yourself Technique and see where it would take him.

James used the following guidelines for himself:

1. He would stop eating when only half the food on his plate was eaten. (James ate out a lot, so this target was primarily for use in restaurants and for the plate

his mother insisted on fixing for him when he visited her. He didn't want to give up this long-standing tradition he and his mother shared.)

2. He would use the Delete Delete Technique when he habitually thought he needed junk food for snacks at work.

3. He would use positive methods for self-soothing, rather than eating, when he felt upset.

4. He would make it a habit to reflect on a time when he was thinner and healthier and recognize how that felt in his body. He would bring those thoughts up consistently throughout the day.

5. He would walk to work three times a week and do some weight training each day before bed.

6. He would go to bed when he was tired instead of dozing off while he watched television late into the evening.

7. When getting home from work in the evening, instead of diving into dinner as soon as he walked in the door, he would eat a piece of fruit and wait to enjoy a meal with his family.

By the time James came back the next week for his session, he had lost 7 pounds. He was excited and proud. James reported that at no time in the previous week had he felt deprived. He ate when he was hungry but did not eat when he was not. When he was stressed, he used his Inner-Smile Technique instead of reaching for food.

James admitted that, one morning that week, he had gotten into an argument with his wife and had been late for work because of traffic. When he did finally get to work, there were donuts on the counter. James picked one up and had it half eaten before he became aware of what he was doing. James immediately stopped eating it and threw the donut away.

James was able to focus on the "progress, not perfection" principle. If he had used his old way of thinking, he would have just finished the donut, telling himself, "What the hell. I already started eating it anyway."

In just that first week, James reported he felt much better than he had in years. He could see that having a wide definition of success took off a lot of the pressure. Without the pressure, he was more likely to be successful.

It's Time for Action

I'm always surprised when I talk to people who put time and effort into planning vacations but don't really give much thought to their everyday life and the inevitable changes that come with it. The definition of life is change, and the quality of our lives dramatically increases when we can experience those changes from a more positive and empowered perspective. Rather than let your life define you, define your life today! Whether you start small or bust through the gate at full speed, take responsibility and step into the next best version of yourself.

Chapter 11

Forgiveness Is the Gift You Give Yourself

The Aramaic word for forgive means to untie. When we refuse to forgive, we keep ourselves tied to painful incidents and relationships. What's more, when we refuse to forgive, we aren't hurting the person who has hurt us, we are hurting ourselves. We create our own bondage to the painful past and then wonder why we can't be happy or move forward in productive ways. Lack of forgiveness leads to bitterness, never happiness. Forgiveness is not about what you or anyone else deserves, it is about setting yourself free to move forward.

In many cases the person who has hurt you has moved on in life, doesn't care, or may not even know the depths to which you are still hurting. This, of course, is only true if the person you refuse to forgive is someone else. When you refuse to forgive yourself, things are even worse. Refusing to forgive yourself, you create your own spiral of low self-confidence and even self-loathing. In short, you create a self-induced "stuck."

Freedom Begins with Forgiving Yourself

You might remember from Chapter 2 that, in my own journey, I came to understand that, until I learned to forgive myself, I wasn't likely to have the peace, happiness, and connection I longed for. Even as I had blamed circumstances and others for my problems, I had blamed myself for not being good enough, for not working hard enough, and for making bad choices. I had catalogued nearly every mistake, big and small, real and perceived, that I had ever made. I had allowed myself to believe that mistakes and bad choices were evidence that I was a bad person, undeserving of happiness. This belief was never true. Mistakes and bad choices are the human condition, even the path to learning and growth.

As you read this chapter, make a commitment to forgive yourself. Apply the Forgiveness Technique to others—and to yourself. Although it will be painful to look at past mistakes, broken relationships, and even intentional wrongdoing, this is the path forward. You have the ability to grieve your past, release it, and move ahead. Take all the time you need, because self-forgiveness is the ultimate gift you give yourself.

Forgiveness Is a Door to a Positive Future

Think about forgiveness as a door to a different kind of life—one of more peace, happiness, and closure. Sometimes the door is very small. You have to crawl through it. Sometimes the threshold to get through that door is lined with shards of glass that cause even more pain. Sometimes the door seems too hard even to find. Trust that the door is there. You may have to search for it, the process will likely be at least uncomfortable or maybe even outright painful, but the door is there.

We all know someone who has allowed the pain of being hurt to turn into a bitterness that permeates every aspect of the person's life. Bitterness robs the person of happiness and the possibility of peace and love. Bitterness can seemingly end a life, long before the person actually takes the last physical breath.

Each of us must decide whether to forgive the person or persons who have most hurt us. In my personal life of almost 50 years, I have known people whose refusal to forgive even seemingly small transgressions has ruined families and created unsaid heartache. I have also had the gift of knowing people who have extended forgiveness with a grace that astonishes. Forgiveness can be one of the most difficult processes to go through, but it is worth it.

Before I began my own journey of growth and change, I kept a mental list of people who had done me wrong. I could easily list all the reasons why these people did not deserve my forgiveness. I was adamant. I did not embrace the news that forgiveness

Chapter 11
Forgiveness Is the Gift You Give Yourself

would be necessary to find the peace and happiness I so desired. I resisted. Over time I surrendered, but I often went kicking and screaming. Today, when I am being honest and vulnerable, I recognize that there is still work to do. I may never have checked off my entire mental list, but I do not regret the work in forgiveness that I have done. I dig deep to find the grace to continue it.

You'll remember from a past chapter that school was a special kind of hell for me. That hell was made all the worse by a teacher I will call Mr. Chuck. As a 10-year-old girl, I could notice the vibe that Mr. Chuck detested me. It's not necessary to believe that I had any kind of special psychic powers to notice this vibe. Mr. Chuck did little to hide it. In fact, he flaunted it!

I arrived in Mr. Chuck's classroom a mess, not knowing the multiplication tables and leaving a trail of lost assignments from locker to desk. Let's not forget: A sprinkling of staring spells and an occasional instance of falling to the floor (seizures) rounded out our time together. I was no teacher's "dream date," but Mr. Chuck saw me as a special kind of "ugly date."

Mr. Chuck would share, sometimes with the whole class, his belief that I was dumb and lazy. He seemed to enjoy laying out on the board a multistep, long-division math problem or a sentence that needed diagramming and asking me to demonstrate how to do it. Mr. Chuck and I both knew that water had a better chance of freezing in hell than I had of completing such a task.

I have no idea how long I stood in front of that class on any occasion. (I couldn't read an analog clock.) I do know it felt like hours. Sometimes Mr. Chuck would even move on to another lesson and complete it while I was still at the board.

I was raised with the threat that, if you cried and upset an adult, you would "get something to really cry about," so I put my skill of stifling tears to a lot of use in Mr. Chuck's class. I had so much anxiety that I developed a coping mechanism of compulsively counting to 24 nearly every waking minute. This only magnified my learning problems, because I couldn't focus on much else. I added, subtracted, and multiplied almost anything from bathroom tiles, to windowpanes, to cars on the road. At night, alone in the dark, I would cry myself to sleep.

As luck would have it, when I moved on to the next grade, Mr. Chuck was reassigned, so I had him again. After two years with Mr. Chuck, by the age of 12, I contemplated suicide even though I didn't fully understand what that meant. My years with Mr. Chuck magnified everything I feared and hated about school. They magnified the shame I felt about not being good enough in life in general. As I looked back, I realized those years were an important juncture. Mr. Chuck's behavior was a significant factor in my decision, consciously or unconsciously, to quit trying. I was never fully able to embrace learning again until I went to college, many years later.

As an adult, when I studied my list of people I needed to forgive, Mr. Chuck was in the top 10. My years with Mr. Chuck had tamped down any confidence or shred of self-dignity I had by the age of 10, which hadn't been much to begin with. Until well into my 30s, just thinking of Mr. Chuck made me want to cry and curl up in the fetal position. The idea of forgiving him, at first, seemed almost repulsive. Just visualizing Mr. Chuck made my skin crawl. I could clearly see, however, that I was suffering because of all the anger I felt toward Mr. Chuck.

At the same time, I felt confident that Mr. Chuck wouldn't even recognize me if I walked right up to him. If he did recognize me, I was willing to bet, his opinion of me wouldn't have changed. With what little objectivity I could muster, I could clearly see that refusing to forgive Mr. Chuck and hanging onto all that hurt was only hurting me.

Although I don't enjoy journaling, I wrote many pages in the process of forgiving Mr. Chuck. As I began to write about him and my experiences in those two years, I got in touch with many feelings and insights that had been suppressed. In the year before Mr. Chuck was my teacher, I remembered seeing him around the school. Intuitively, I always sensed something about him that I didn't understand. Something wasn't good, and I knew he tried to hide it.

Chapter 11
Forgiveness Is the Gift You Give Yourself

Mr. Chuck was uptight, fastidious, and avoided direct eye contact with most adults and many of the kids. Alarm bells went off for me around Mr. Chuck, even as a young child. Because of my age, self-doubt, and fear, I didn't understand or value my insights.

Years later, as I wrote in my journal, it struck me that Mr. Chuck was a closet homosexual. This was 1976 in rural Pennsylvania. Being a homosexual man would likely have been a terrible burden.

I want to be clear here. I am not attributing Mr. Chuck's negative behaviors to being gay. Plenty of straight men and women are uptight, fastidious, and avoid eye contact. A gay man is no more likely to treat a child the way Mr. Chuck treated me than a straight man would. In fact, the following year, in a much different way, I had another male teacher who was as glaringly abusive as Mr. Chuck was, and he most certainly was not gay.

Looking back as an adult, it was obvious to me that Mr. Chuck was suffering with his own personal hell. Although this is not an excuse, it is probably a factor that contributed to how he chose to treat me. Let's face it, happy, well-adjusted people don't treat anyone as Mr. Chuck treated me.

I wanted to talk to Mr. Chuck as part of my process, but trying to find him proved impossible. He had left teaching, but no one at the school would tell me where he had gone. Several years later, I discovered that he had been forced out of teaching because of charges of "endangering the welfare of a child, corruption of a minor (two boys), and indecent assault."

During my forgiveness process, I had another flash about Mr. Chuck. I could suddenly see that—in my struggle with feelings of shame, regret, insecurity, and lack of self-love—I was not alone. He and I probably had some of that in common. The difference is that I was an innocent child, with no choices or resources, who wasn't doing anything wrong; he was an adult doing many things wrong. As I said earlier, no self-respecting adult would treat anyone as he treated me; he was not a self-respecting adult. Self-loathing, shame, fear, and regret were probably Mr. Chuck's close companions. That being said, what he did to me and any other victims was wrong. I'm not implying there are any excuses for Mr. Chuck's abusive behaviors. Forgiving is not condoning, forgetting, or ignoring. However, I have been able to forgive and find compassion for Mr. Chuck. Standing in his shoes made my shoes feel damn comfortable.

Today when I think about Mr. Chuck and other people who have hurt me, in large and small ways, I can almost always find some forgiveness and, with that, peace and freedom in my own life.

The Forgiveness Technique, which follows, may help you find peace and freedom. Unlike some of the other techniques in this book, the Forgiveness Technique is not linear and straightforward. Forgiveness is highly personal. It can involve a process that unfolds, sometimes slowly.

The Forgiveness Technique

1. Write out, as fully and completely as possible, what happened from your perspective.
2. Be as objective as possible. If you are struggling with objectivity, try using the Peel-Away-the-Story Technique. If you need this technique, refer back to Chapter 6.
3. Try to imagine yourself as the person who hurt you. What perspectives might this person have had that are different from your own?
4. Try to be compassionate to the other person; imagine yourself as him or her. What could have driven this person's behavior: fear, self-hatred, self-loathing, or a mental health issue? Ask yourself, "Would I trade places with the person who hurt me?" Most often, the answer is no.
5. Make a list, if possible, of any good things that came out of the experience. Dig deep; was there an unseen benefit?

6. If your hurt goes back a long way and you feel a strong resistance to forgiving, ask yourself if you are getting a payoff by refusing to forgive. Examples of payoffs include getting to feel superior, being comfortable in the role of victim, using what happened as an excuse not to take action and be responsible for your own life, or using your lack of forgiveness as leverage over the person who hurt you. If you have resistance to forgiving, discovering the payoff is a vital step. Do not take this step lightly!

7. Make a commitment to stop telling the story of what happened. When we continue to tell the story, we energize the incident and keep the pain alive. Forgiveness is about letting it go, and you can't let it go if you keep repeating the story.

8. If appropriate, shift your focus to the person who has hurt you. This step can be useful in cases such as painful break-ups, divorce, or close family or friend relationships. Too often it is easy to focus on the hurt or wrongdoing and disregard the positive attributes the other person has or the good times or the accomplishments you shared.

9. Practice listing three positive things about the person who has hurt you. If it was a person with whom you had a personal relationship, what attracted you in the first place? If you are struggling, notice how people who haven't been hurt by that person perceive him or her. If you did not have a personal relationship or you did not choose to have the person in your life, consider that someone loves/cares for the person. Everyone is someone's son/daughter, mother/father, sibling, or friend. No one can be all bad, everyone has some good. Make it your job to find the good—not for the person's sake, but for yours.

10. Wish the person who has hurt you well. You don't have to see the person or communicate your well wishes; do this in your own process. You may have to take baby steps initially, but I have faith you can do it.

11. Recognize that, at the very least, you know you can live through what happened. You already have! You may realize you are stronger than you thought.

12. Know that forgiveness is a decision. You choose to let go of resentment and thoughts of revenge and to put effort into moving forward positively in your life.

13. Give yourself permission and time to process your pain and emotions. Do not try to suppress your feelings. What we resist persists. The goal is to let the pain go so you can have freedom. Suppressed emotions do not equal freedom.

14. Be patient and forgiving of yourself. Remember, the technique is for progress, not perfection. There is no magic wand, and forgiveness is personal. As long as you make a goal to forgive, you are making progress even if it doesn't always feel like it.

15. Use the Setting-an-Intention Technique (Chapter 7) and the Heart-Centered Breathing Technique (Chapter 8) to *visualize*, *feel*, and *experience* yourself becoming untied from this most painful experience.

16. Get a clear picture: Forgiveness does not mean you forget or approve of what happened. Forgiving someone does not mean that you will trust him or her in the future. This is an important distinction, because the balance of trust, wisdom, and appropriateness can be challenging. If you truly forgive someone, you can move on, but moving on doesn't necessarily mean you trust or even want a relationship or even contact with the person.

My client Sam was mugged as she made her way to her car after work one night. She suffered a concussion and a fractured ankle. Sam struggled in the days and months after the attack, as her physical injuries required adjustments to her routines and caused considerable pain. Although Sam had never considered herself a fearful person, she developed fears about working late and getting to her car. She naturally had a lot of anger toward her attacker. She fantasized about the attacker spending years in jail, paying for what he had done.

Eventually Sam's attacker was caught. She learned he had grown up in foster care, had a long history of drug addiction, was uneducated, and had no marketable skills and no family. Sam's own cousin had struggled with drug addiction for years before finally getting clean. Sam had always had compassion for her cousin and his family. She had seen firsthand what addiction was like for them. Like Sam's attacker, Sam's cousin had stolen and made countless bad choices. The difference was that Sam's cousin had always had a family who loved and supported him. Because of this, he had the opportunity to return to school and get his life back on track.

After Sam learned her attacker's story, she was able to find her way to more compassion and less anger. Her concussion was probably not going to have a long-term effect. She might develop arthritis in her ankle as she aged, but her problems were clearly more desirable then those of her attacker. Sam was able to see the struggles with addiction her attacker faced, juxtapose those against her own cousin's addiction struggles, and recognize what distinguished her attacker from her cousin were a loving family and opportunities.

After Sam worked through her process, she recognized she would not take any joy from knowing that her attacker was sitting in prison, paying for his mistakes. She recognized also that what he had done was certainly wrong and that he should pay the consequences. In the end, her attacker went to jail. Sam wasn't his only victim. Sam doesn't know where her attacker is or how he is doing, but she wishes him well. Each time Sam thinks about the night she was mugged and the likelihood that her ankle may give her trouble, she makes it a point to be grateful that her cousin is still clean and living a successful life.

When You Are the One Who Needs to Be Forgiven

As humans, we all make mistakes and hurt others, sometimes accidentally and sometimes intentionally. If you are truly sorry, asking for forgiveness can be a powerful release so that both parties can move on. Asking for forgiveness requires humility, vulnerability, and the acknowledgment of weakness or wrongdoing. Trying to negate your wrongdoing by blaming circumstances or the other person is not the same as asking for forgiveness.

When you are truly sorry for what you have done, take steps to repair the damage you have caused. This includes a sincere apology in which you take full responsibility for what happened. You must promise to make every effort not to repeat the behavior or similar behaviors.

Forgiveness is a process, so you must be willing to give the other person time to heal and regain trust in you. Depending upon the situation, you, and the other person(s) involved, the process can be relatively short or one that takes months or years.

Years ago I attended a funeral in my hometown and ran into an old boyfriend, Stan, and his girlfriend. The girlfriend seemed committed to Stan. She had moved with him following his last promotion at work, and she seemed to love him. I asked Stan if he thought they would eventually marry. Stan quickly replied, "Oh, I could never remarry. I got married once, and my wife treated me so badly. She made me afraid of the institution of marriage. I could never do it again." Asked how long Stan had been divorced, he answered, "Ten years."

Now there was a good reason he was an ex-boyfriend—no one ever classified this guy as a catch. Yet it was obvious that Stan placed all the blame for his failed marriage on his former wife, leaving no room to examine his role in the broken relationship.

When you refuse to move on or forgive, like Stan, you allow your life to be defined, in part, by what happened. You rob yourself of an opportunity to grow and change with your life experiences. Stan's lack of forgiveness and his refusal to acknowledge his own responsibility in the relationship had him permanently stuck. Perhaps Stan refused to look objectively at the relationship because he was afraid he might have to forgive himself.

This example brings us full circle to the beginning of the chapter. Often, the freedom to become unstuck only comes with self-forgiveness.

CIRCLE BACK TO YOURSELF

In Chapter 12, I outline an exercise that involves writing a series of letters. If you struggle with self-forgiveness, go to that section. Follow the instructions to write a letter to yourself as you were during the time you made the mistake for which you want to forgive yourself. Then follow the instructions to write a letter to your future self about how life is different now that you have forgiven yourself.

Try to see yourself as you would see someone you love. Treat yourself the way you would treat that other person. Would you find it easier to forgive, to be more compassionate, and to want that other person to be happy?

Imagine sitting down and having a loving compassionate discussion about what happened with you. Even give yourself a warm embrace and use the Heart-Centered Breathing Technique as you *visualize*, *feel*, and *experience* yourself being forgiven.

It's Time for Action

Self-acceptance and love can be hard-won accomplishments, but they are your most important ones. When you engage in self-forgiveness, self-acceptance, and self-love, life gets better not only for you, but for those you love and for whom you care. Begin forgiving yourself today and reap the benefits. Benefits include healthier relationships, less stress and anxiety, improved psychological and spiritual well-being, and less risk of drug and alcohol abuse. Traversing that doorway to forgive might not be easy, but it is the right choice.

Give yourself the gift of forgiveness starting now!

CHAPTER 12

CAP IT OFF WITH CONFIDENCE

DR. JOE RUBINO, author of *The Self-Esteem Book: The Ultimate Guide to Boost the Most Underrated Ingredient for Success and Happiness in Life*, suggests that 85% of the world's population is affected by low self-esteem. In addition, according to the organization Confidence Coalition, only 2% of women think they are beautiful. From an objective standpoint, more than 2% of the women out there are beauties. Of course, beauty is in the eye of the beholder, and most women clearly don't behold themselves as beautiful.

Based on these statistics, if you struggle with confidence, you certainly are not alone. The good news is that confidence can be approached much like any skill—yes, confidence is a matter of perspective and skill!

This chapter is full of information and techniques to increase your confidence. Some of the techniques involve an investment of time, and some are quick-and-dirty confidence boosters to give you a shot of confidence right when you need it. Digesting the material in this chapter and completing the exercises will be worth your effort because your level of confidence (or lack of the same) influences your entire life.

The pervasiveness of low self-confidence not only undermines individuals like you and me, it has high social costs. People struggling with self-confidence are unlikely to live to their full potential and capitalize on their talents. If 85% of us aren't expressing our talents, our society is wasting a lot of talent.

In addition, low self-confidence is a contributing factor in expensive social issues, such as school dropout, teen pregnancy, and crime. I'm guessing there is an excessive amount of bravado in prisons but not much real confidence.

In families, low self-confidence shows up in drug and alcohol abuse, domestic violence, bullying, and personal debt associated with the need to buy things to feel better about oneself. Low self-confidence is often at the root of anger, depression, and suicide.

People lacking confidence on the inside often try to find confidence on the outside. The effort might include a relationship with someone who seems to validate the person's worth. The effort might involve overpowering or bullying others so the person can feel powerful and superior. It might involve any number of destructive practices used to mask the pain of a poor sense of self-worth.

When we don't feel good about ourselves, we don't expect much out of life. As a result, we settle for relationships that, at best, fail to nurture us and, at worst, are abusive physically, emotionally, and spiritually. We may stay stuck in jobs that suck the life out of us in exchange for a paycheck that may or may not even be fair. The biggest price we pay, however, is the ever-present sense of unhappiness we feel.

Shift Your Focus and You'll Shift Your Life

If you struggle with confidence, it's most likely because of faulty focus, thinking, and/or beliefs. In other words, you struggle because you view yourself inaccurately. Most likely, your perception of yourself is skewed to the negative. Chances are you have developed a habit of identifying with failures, setbacks, embarrassing situations, or a personal history of put-down messages.

This chapter is all about changing your self-perception so you can enjoy the confidence you deserve and a self-image that is more accurate than the one you currently hold.

In my work, one of the biggest misconceptions I come across is that people with high self-confidence don't struggle or fail. The truth is that everyone has struggles and experiences failure. Here is the big difference between those with high and those with low self-confidence: People with high self-confidence focus on improving themselves

Chapter 12
Cap It Off with Confidence

and their lives; those with low self-confidence are caught up in trying to avoid mistakes or failures.

This important distinction in perception can make or break you in the arena of confidence. Moving toward improvement is a positive goal; focusing on avoiding mistakes or failing is rooted in the negative. As we've seen in earlier chapters, you attract what you think.

What's more, in the face of failure, those with high self-confidence view any failure as an isolated event, an opportunity to learn. Those with low self-confidence see failure as a judgment upon themselves. In the face of any single failure, these people believe they are failures. Then they act out the belief. They attract failure.

Shifting our feelings and perceptions about failure is a major step toward seeing ourselves more accurately and attracting more of what we want.

It is impossible to live without failure. There are no guaranteed outcomes in life, and we almost never have all the information; there are simply too many variables in life to know everything. All anyone can do is work with the information available and make his or her best judgment.

For example, imagine you are trying to choose between two very similar jobs. You can do research; consider the compensation packages; and then prioritize variables such as distance from home, work environment, etc.

You might make a good choice and start working, only to discover that the owner had decided to sell or relocate. Since you had no way of knowing this information, seeing your job choice as a failure is inaccurate. You considered all the information available to you, but you didn't have access to additional information that could affect you. In this example, your choice isn't due to failure. It is due to a change in circumstances outside your control.

EXAMINE YOUR CHOICES TO LEARN ABOUT YOURSELF

A second example, although more subjective, is potentially more powerful to the work of real change. This example identifies an important element of true self-confidence: knowing yourself and the deep reasons behind your choices.

Imagine you begin dating someone who seems perfect for you. You get married or involved in a long-term relationship. Only later do you discover your partner is dishonest or a cheater. Looking back, you see clues or red flags you disregarded or did not want to acknowledge.

In this example, you did not take into account all the available information or clues that this person was dishonest or had a wandering eye. You may have chosen to filter out the clues because they did not fit the paradigm of how you wanted to view the person. Maybe your desire for the relationship trumped the information or clues available.

In this case, examining and learning about the relationship provides an opportunity to learn and grow. Examining why you chose to ignore the clues and why you felt you needed this relationship can be a powerful exercise, leading to real change. If you were willing to turn a blind eye or excuse this person's behaviors, you now have an opportunity to discover the underlying beliefs you have about yourself—the beliefs that led you to commit to an unhealthy relationship.

Potential questions to ask include

- Did I feel I wouldn't find a better potential mate?
- Was I concerned about what others may have thought?
- Was I more invested in an image than I was with my own best interests?
- Was fear a potential factor in my choosing to be with this person? (Was I afraid of being alone, not being able to take care of myself, etc.?)

When you have chosen poorly in an important relationship or life direction, ask yourself serious questions like these and carefully examine the answers. Go a step

Chapter 12
Cap It Off with Confidence

further and tie those answers back to root feelings, beliefs, and expectations. This process allows you to learn from your mistakes and increase your self-awareness. Such knowledge leads to natural confidence and better future choices.

Experts say that the best indicator of future behavior is past behaviors. With insight and change, you can prove the experts wrong. After you have learned about yourself or the root beliefs that were driving you, you can change the behaviors that contributed to the problem. Examining and taking responsibility for your own choices is a key to growth. Simply blaming the other person won't really help you; in fact, blaming will hinder your own growth or keep you stuck.

Relationships provide powerful learning opportunities because in our relationships we play out our insecurities, fears, beliefs, and unresolved issues. It would be wonderful if people only got into relationships with people who shared their values and goals, enjoyed mutual respect, and nurtured one another. The truth is that people get into relationships for a whole host of unhealthy reasons rooted in low self-confidence. When you struggle with low confidence, you are prone to be in a relationship with someone who makes you feel validated; fuels your insecurities; or meets your perceived need to be in a relationship because being alone is simply too painful, scary, embarrassing, or proves you are a loser.

For example, consider a man who won't consider dating a woman who isn't younger, blond, and fits his idea of "hot." This man is playing out his need to be validated or perceived in a certain way. His commitment to the relationship is all about him and his need for the validation the relationship can offer. These narrow parameters for potential partners are based on his faulty perception that he needs a certain kind of woman to be viewed positively by others or to feel a certain way.

Also consider a woman who is only interested in men in a certain profession, such as doctors. This woman may feel the need to achieve status by her husband's profession. Her desire to be with a doctor may reflect the belief that she is not good enough on her own.

Knowing yourself is the key to natural confidence (as well as making good choices). Take the time to invest in getting to understand who you are and why you make certain choices repeatedly. Explore and challenge your underlying beliefs, expectations, and histories. Without this work, real confidence will evade you. It's too easy to look to people and circumstances outside yourself for validation of your faulty beliefs about yourself or for excuses to explain why you don't measure up to your own standards. Invest the time to dig deep into self-awareness and reap the rewards.

Practice Confidence-Building Exercises

Examining your choices and the underlying feelings that drive them allows you to make real changes that lead to confidence. Although real change is possible, habits die hard, and situations will come up that shake your confidence. For those times, this chapter presents confidence-building exercises that will help you shift in ways that honestly, appropriately, and truthfully reflect who you are. These exercises will place you squarely on the path of true confidence.

Write Six Important Letters

In the spirit of building confidence, write six distinct letters to help you let go, move forward, release a burden, say good-bye to a fear, and build love and respect for yourself. This might seem a tall order. But with a bit of soul-searching and an open mind, you will find you step a little lighter and feel a little better. Each letter will help you build confidence. For the most part, whether or not you mail these letters will make little difference. The power is in the work it takes to write them.

1. Write a letter to yourself as a young child.

    Choose a time in your childhood that was particularly difficult. For some people the quandary will be which time to choose, there were so many. Others, who experienced happier childhoods, may have to dig deep. Either way the effort is worth it.

Get a clear picture of yourself at this stage of childhood. Address the younger you, expressing compassion, sympathy, and love. Let your younger self know that you now understand how he or she is hurting. Let the child know he or she is neither at fault nor deserving of what is happening. Let the child know that things will get better and explain that he or she will be okay. In the letter, give that child the love and comfort you may have needed but didn't receive.

2. Write a letter to someone who hurt you.

The purpose of this letter is to help you release the bonds that tie you to something or someone from your past. The release allows you to move forward in the best possible way for yourself.

In this letter, express whatever forgiveness you can. Explain that your forgiveness does not mean what this person did was all right, but rather that you accept that the incident happened and you are letting go for yourself so that you can have peace.

Too often I hear people express doubt about forgiving those who hurt them. They fear letting the other person off the hook for what he or she has done. They fear being too generous to the person who hurt them. This is faulty thinking: Forgiveness is a gift you give yourself so you are free to leave the past in the past rather than let it rob you of your happiness, empowerment, and confidence today and in the future.

A very wise friend, Kathi, is fond of saying, "Withholding forgiveness is like swallowing poison and waiting for the other person to die." The anger connected with withholding forgiveness is toxic and further empowers the person or situation that hurt us to continue to inflict pain.

3. Write a letter to a fear you want to release.

    Write this letter as you would to an individual (Dear Fear of _____) to whom you are saying good-bye. No hard feelings—your time together has simply ended. Thank your fear for being there when you thought you needed it, but acknowledge that your relationship to this fear no longer serves you. The fear is now just a burden holding you back. Say good-bye with no hard feelings. This is just a natural ending of a relationship you no longer need.

4. Write a letter to someone who is no longer in your life.

    The person may no longer be in your life because of divorce, estrangement, or a painful end to a relationship. The person might be someone who has died, with whom you have unfinished business.

    In this letter, reflect on the genuine good times you shared and acknowledge that, even though the relationship ended badly, it brought good times and happiness to you as well. Let the individual know what you appreciate about him or her.

    When a relationship ends, it is easy to label that relationship as bad and not take into account the positive or happy times you had. This one-sided thinking polarizes and skews perceptions. This letter helps you to resolve the bad and balance your feelings about the relationship.

5. Write a letter to yourself.

    The purpose of this letter is to express love, respect, or admiration for an area of your life where you have done well, overcome adversity, or learned from your mistakes. Formulate this letter as though you are writing it to a friend or loved one to express just how impressive this person has been. This letter helps you shift your current perspective about yourself to one that is more rooted in accuracy.

6. Write a letter to your future self.

    You can write this letter to your future self who will be alive a month from now or a year from now; the time frame is up to you. A letter to your future self is a good way to remind yourself how far you've come and to hold yourself accountable for the progress you plan to make. Sign and seal the letter to your future self and then date it for opening at an appropriate time in your future. Or consider using the online service Futureme.org, which will email your letter to you on the date you designate.

If you write these letters—and include some heart and soul—you will have more peace, comfort, and closure about your past as well as a deeper love and respect for yourself. These all lead to more self-confidence. As I said earlier, except for the letter to your future self, mailing or not mailing these letters makes little difference. The power is in the work it takes to write them.

Don't Pole-Vault the Mouse Turds

We often waste a precious resource, time, by making issues bigger than they need to be. Worse yet, we fuss over things we simply cannot change. I call this behavior pole-vaulting over mouse turds. Such behaviors undermine confidence, foster self-doubt, and contribute to feelings of fear or dependency. Here are four steps to avoid pole-vaulting over mouse turds.

1. Make a decision to change something, and just do it!

    Do it now. Small changes, like cleaning a drawer or organizing some files, not only start momentum, they provide a sense of control and accomplishment. If you can't make a change now, make a game plan and implement the plan sooner rather than later.

2. Accept the things that are simply outside your control.

   Stop fussing about things like the weather, traffic, and the behaviors of another person. Accept what you cannot change and move on. This frees up your emotional energy to make real changes where you can—in your own thoughts and behaviors.

3. Look at the big picture and take a longer view of things.

   Ask yourself, "Is the thing I am upset about today really going to matter in 5 days, 5 years, or even 5 hours?" If not, let it go.

4. Examine your focus.

   Ask yourself, "What am I focusing on that simply is not working?" Then change your approach. This empowers you, and empowerment leads to confidence because you know you can make a difference in your own life.

Develop the Gratitude Habit

Gratitude builds positive momentum and focuses our attention on what's right in our lives. When things seem to be going wrong, the practice of gratitude can seem counterintuitive, but gratitude is one of the quickest ways to turn things around.

Try keeping a gratitude journal. If journaling isn't your thing, at least keep a running list of things for which you are grateful. Get into the habit of closing out your day by listing five things for which you are genuinely grateful. This is a positive and confidence-building way to end your day.

Be specific as you express gratitude. For example, go beyond simple appreciation for your home. Express gratitude for the wall color that makes you happy or the comfortable sofa that provides a place to snuggle with loved ones. Paying attention to small details increases the impact of your gratitude.

Chapter 12
Cap It Off with Confidence

Be grateful for yourself and the things you do well. For example, be grateful for your talents. When someone gives you a compliment, appreciate the compliment. Also be grateful for the talent, skill, or behavior that prompted the compliment.

For even more power, engage in gratitude projects. My friend Lori's mother died a few years ago, and Lori continues to miss her every day. The Christmas after her mother passed, Lori began the tradition of giving hummingbird-themed gifts as a way to commemorate her mother and her love of hummingbirds.

One year, in her mother's honor, Lori designed gratitude journals to give friends and family. She used quotes contributed by friends and family members in the design. Those included in the project were honored and carefully considered the quotes they submitted. I know searching for the right quote made me slow down, think, and reflect on all the things for which I can be grateful.

On the inside cover of the journal, Lori memorialized her mother and included a note about her mother's love of life and gratitude. Lori's gratitude-journal gift touched many lives, and it allowed Lori to express gratitude for her mother. Lori's gratitude project provided a powerful outlet for sharing, which is the highest expression of love and gratitude.

Wrap Yourself in Love, Appreciation, and Acceptance for 30 Days

Make a commitment: Every day for 30 days, focus on and list five things you love, appreciate, respect, or like about yourself. Studies show that engaging in a behavior consistently for 30 days lays the groundwork for a habit. This exercise helps you make gratitude a healthy habit.

If you struggle with this one, try seeing yourself from another person's perspective. For example, think about how someone who loves you experiences your best qualities. You might see yourself through the eyes of a child, spouse, friend, or parent. If you struggle with confidence at work, imagine how a client or colleague with whom you have had success perceives you.

The intentional focus and act of writing five things you love, appreciate, and respect about yourself create a shift and help build a positive lifelong habit of appreciating yourself.

GIVE YOURSELF THE OPPORTUNITY TO BE SUCCESSFUL SOONER VERSUS LATER

Commit to accomplishing something small in the short term. This will build your confidence to take on bigger challenges for change. Your project can be something as simple as spending an hour each day organizing a closet, drawer, or area in your home or office. Completing short projects is a great way to get instant feedback and see results. Success creates a positive confidence cycle and motivates you to do more.

If you have an idea for a business, nonprofit, or other venture but haven't been moving forward, try starting a blog or discussion board to get your feet wet and build momentum. If you have a particular interest, reach out to a like-minded community to learn more, build relationships, and share ideas. Meetup.com is a great online resource for more interests than I can list here. If you go to the website and type in an interest (for example, entrepreneurship or scrapbooking) or challenge (for example, social anxiety or shyness), you are likely to discover an active group of like-minded people who get together often.

Get out there and do *something*. Trying new things and stepping outside your comfort zone will help you build confidence.

LET IT GO: DON'T LET EXCESSIVE STUFF WEIGH YOU DOWN

We have an energy connection with everything we own and every relationship in which we are engaged. When we are overwhelmed with the chaos of stuff and let our energy be zapped by relationships that no longer fit (or maybe never did), it is hard to feel confident and energized.

Chapter 12
Cap It Off with Confidence

With this in mind, take an inventory of your life, including possessions, physical spaces, your car, and relationships. It makes sense to keep the connection with nice things that bring you pleasure, have a useful purpose in life, or sentimental value. Consider letting go of the stuff that takes up valuable physical and emotional space.

Seek to become more discerning about what to keep and what to let go with grace and dignity.

Your work with this book marks a new beginning and a new way of being in your life. A cleaning-house approach to life is a necessary step to moving forward. Consider trying my Three-Bag Exercise.

- Designate three bags: one bag for stuff that has no value for anyone, a second for things that still have value but are no longer useful to you, and a third for things about whose value you are unsure. Move through your space, putting things in the appropriate bags.
- When you are done, tie up the third bag and place it out of the way—maybe in your garage, basement, or in the back of a closet. Make a note on your calendar or phone to open the bag one year from now.
- The following year, if you have not opened that third bag to get something, don't open it. Just throw the bag out. If an item has meaning to you, you will want it or need it within a year's time.

When getting rid of things, start small. For example, throw out every pen that doesn't write, all the old mail and papers that aren't important, the dried-up hand sanitizers and lotions in your car console, ratty shoes that aren't going to see the light of day again, and anything else in that category. Then move on to bigger things. Come to terms with clothes that haven't fit or weren't appropriate for two consecutive years, and the water bowl belonging to the dog who died a year ago.

If you are like most people, making small changes will energize you. You will then find it easier to tackle the big stuff. Making changes frees up your energy and contributes to feeling better, which lends itself to feeling more confident. Feelings of confidence lead to even bigger changes and more confidence in a positive upward spiral.

Quick-and-Dirty Confidence-Building Exercises

The mind-body connection is very powerful. We can influence our minds with our bodies to experience confidence when we need it. Here are five quick ways to use your body to increase your confidence right now!

1. Stand akimbo.

    Stand with your feet shoulder-width apart, elbows bent, and hands on your hips with fingers in the front and thumbs in the back. Strange as it may seem, standing akimbo automatically makes us feel more confident. It's a power stance.

    Power stances have been associated with low levels of cortisol (the stress hormone) and high levels of testosterone (associated with confidence and dominance). Research shows that just 2 minutes of akimbo stance can give you a mental jolt of confidence. The body's position changes your brain's mind about yourself.

2. Take up more space.

    Whether sitting or standing, confident people tend to take up more space than others do. Less confident people are likely to make themselves seem smaller by folding in on themselves: slumping shoulders, slouching, and keeping their feet close together.

    Stand up straight, shoulders back, head up, and feet hip distance apart. When you take up more space, you feel more confident. Once again, your body gives your brain a message of confidence.

3. Smile.

   When you smile, the brain gets the message that you are happy and releases positive endorphins that contribute to feelings of happiness. This creates a positive-feedback loop between the body and mind. This is a prime example of how "fake it until you make it" can work.

   Even holding a pencil between your teeth for 2 minutes can send the "I am happy" message to your brain. Smiling brings positive energy that helps you see and think more expansively.

4. Reflect on an experience of success.

   Remember that the mind makes very little distinction between what is happening in real time and what we vividly hold in the mind's eye. By focusing on a past success, you will experience an increase in your feelings of success in real time.

5. Expose yourself to humor.

   When we laugh, we send feel-good chemicals cascading down from the brain. When we feel better, we do better, and that leads to confidence. Exposing yourself to humor for just a few minutes has positive results. So on your phone, bookmark a few quick videos that are good for a reliable laugh, and see what a difference humor makes.

It's Time for Action

Experience has taught me that low self-confidence is typically a perception issue. Typically, people simply don't see themselves accurately. They base their personal value on misinformation, faulty perceptions, past failures, other people's opinions, or the story they tell themselves about the past.

As you work through the techniques and exercises in this chapter, you will begin to experience more confidence and find it easier and easier to learn to love, appreciate, and accept yourself. This leads to the real confidence that everyone desires.

Take note: Growing in confidence is about shifting perspectives and making progress. Life is constantly changing, and on some days it may seem like self-doubt is winning out. On those days, do the best you can with this chapter, get a good night's sleep, and expect tomorrow to be at least a little bit better. Over time, chances are that tomorrows will get hugely better.

CHAPTER 13

GOOD-BYE FOR NOW—A FEW CLOSING WORDS

As I put the last words to page, I anticipate turning 50 in a few short months. The U-Haul of issues that I carried in life certainly has gotten much lighter in the 20 years since I began this journey. *Progress, not perfection* remains my mantra. Many days are amazing: I feel good, happy, optimistic, and I value the smarts I do have and feel connected to all those I love. Some days though, the old ugly still rears its head.

A few months ago, Larry, Henry, Zane, and I were in San Diego on vacation. On our last night, we went to the beach restaurant at our hotel. We had dined there several times, watching the sunset from the fire-pit table we had come to think of as our own. Although I had requested "our" table for our last night, it was not available. As we sat nearby, discussing what a great trip it had been, we lamented not having our favorite table for our last night.

Suddenly the hostess came over to announce that, since our table had opened up, she was moving us. We happily gathered our things and moved. As we were sitting down, I announced, as I often do, "It always works out."

Suddenly, with a hint of aggravation in his voice, Zane said, "I wish it wouldn't work out because you always say that, and I want you to be wrong. I want it to not work out for once."

My reaction was visceral. I literally felt as if I had been hit in the stomach. I felt this statement to my core. Yes, Zane had been a little sassy and, yes, he wasn't using the manners and respect we expect from the boys, but I was reacting to so much more than to that. I literally felt sick. Suddenly, in that moment, I was overcome with fear that all of our lives might not work out. I was angry with Zane that he could possibly want that to happen to us.

In fact, many times in my life, things hadn't seemed to work out at all. I had had heartbreaking experiences of feeling alone, beginning with my school years and continuing into adulthood. People who were supposed to take care of me had abused me. I had felt stupid and unworthy at home and at school. As a poor single mother, I had sometimes chosen to feed Scott instead of myself. But the biggest, deepest heartbreaks had been during the times when I had no longer felt hope. There were times I had feared, to my core, that things would not work out and that I was going to teeter off the edge of whatever stability I had.

As I looked across the table at Larry and the boys, I felt so much anxiety that I nearly went into a full-blown panic attack. I was gripped with fear that something would happen to Zane or Henry and his life wouldn't work out. I was overwhelmed with fear that we would lose our financial security; that the business I had worked so hard to build would fail; or that something would happen to both Larry and me, leaving the three younger boys alone in the world.

I had all this overwhelming anxiety over an 11-year-old boy's snarky comment. Really?

Thankfully, I realized that, no matter how intense, my fear and anger were unfounded. I quickly used the Delete Delete Technique, the On-Demand Relaxation Technique, and my Inner-Smile Technique to overcome the anxiety and visceral feelings I was experiencing. Within a few minutes, I was feeling much better and could enjoy my evening, but I was still bothered.

I recognized that my fears and anxiety needed to be examined because they reared their ugly heads too easily. Later that evening, I used my Peel-Away-the-Story Technique.

As I worked my way through the technique, I was reminded that things did work out. My happiness today—feeling good, being optimistic, recognizing and valuing my

Chapter 13
Good-Bye for Now—A Few Closing Words

own unique intelligence, the success I have in my business, and being connected to all those I love—all of this for me was born out of the contrast my life has provided me. Unlike Goldie the fish, whose whole life is spent in the comfort of water, my life had provided lots of contrast and discomfort. If I am happy with who I am and where I am today, I have to value and embrace everything that came before it: the good, bad, and—yes, certainly—the ugly.

Over the years, I had worked through many of these ugly issues by using the Peel-Away-the-Story Technique. However, I had never done so when I was so emotional and certainly never when I was surrounded by the perfection of a great vacation. I had never done this work when, in my mind, I should just be happy and relaxed.

Suddenly I recognized that once again I had "should" on myself. Because the vacation was such a great time, I had an unexamined expectation that no bad from the past would be present. I was indignant that the past pain had reared its ugly head at dinner on this wonderful night, of all times.

I worked through the technique, peeling away the story I was telling myself underneath. I realized that the past would always be present simply because it was part of me. The past contributed to the present. I needed to start accepting rather than resisting the experiences that had formed me. The moment I accepted the past, all of it—just as it was—the fear, anxiety, and anger simply fell away. I was reminded again that what we resist persists. What we accept loses its grip.

Shortly after that night on vacation, I made the decision to write this book. I had always said I would write a book before my 50th birthday, and so I returned home and began almost immediately. During the writing process, many issues have come up for me. Sometimes I had writer's block; the words to my own story wouldn't come because I feared I wasn't good enough to write it or my voice didn't matter. I became upset with myself that I had put off writing this book, not making my goals a priority. I experienced anxiety that readers wouldn't find the book helpful and fear that my professional life's work wasn't compelling enough to make a difference in anyone's life.

One day I had mother's guilt when I was irritable because I had worked until 5 a.m. and was running on three hours of sleep. Another day the mother's guilt was there as I was pulling out all the stops to meet a deadline. That day Henry, Zane, and I agreed, without speaking about it, that they could spend the large portion of a day playing video games, violating the one-hour daily allotment.

Often I felt buoyant, confident, and proud to be taking on such a challenging project in a relatively short time. Other times I got weepy as I relived much of what had already been processed and healed, but still hurt when I brought it out to be examined and put into writing.

As you can see, writing this book wasn't easy. At times, it was downright painful. In the process, however, I've come to marvel at how far I've come on my journey. I've also seen that resolving and embracing the past is a lifelong journey—for me as well as for you. Moving forward demands courage, but the results are worth it. None of us has to conquer it all in a day.

It's Time for Action

The techniques in this book allow you to resolve a painful thought, feeling, or experience in quick, easy-to-use steps. That's good news. Now all you have to do is use what you've learned.

You can repair damage you've done to relationships by learning to say *I am sorry*. You can learn to forgive and accept those you love for who they are rather than who or what you may want them to be. More important, you can repair the damage that others have done to you or you have done to yourself. We *do* get second chances and third chances. In fact, we all get a ton of chances to do things differently, every single day.

I encourage you, use the opportunity you have today and move forward to make the changes that are important to you. Don't let your past dictate your future. Don't let your fear and anxiety stop you. Don't give in to limitations and the story that has held you back. Don't worry about tomorrow or put off change until some magical day when

Chapter 13
Good-Bye for Now—A Few Closing Words

starting something new makes sense. Do it today. The longest journey starts with the first step. Take your first step today and lighten your personal U-Haul in life.

No matter where you are on your path, I wish you only the best your life has to offer. Make your own path today.

With love and gratitude,

Coach Monique

Monday, August 18, 2014

Ready Reference Guide for Easy-to-Learn, Easy-to-Use, and Immediately Relevant Techniques

The Delete Delete Technique .... Page 32

This technique will help you build thought awareness so you can recognize and identify negative thinking and speech and then make gentle, non-judgmental corrections. Practicing Delete Delete will help you shift your thought patterns to be more positive, supportive, and successful.

The Simple Meditation Technique .... Page 43

This meditation, using a relaxation response, will allow you to quickly and easily drop down to the meditative level and enjoy all the benefits of meditation in an easy-to-learn format.

If you wish to listen and follow along with the meditation, it is available for download by following these steps:

1. Visit http://www.coachmonique.com.
2. Click the "I Bought the Book, now I need the Simple 20 Minute Mediation Technique Download."
3. Enter the password Iamrelaxed (capital *I*, no spaces).

THE ON-DEMAND RELAXATION TECHNIQUE .... PAGE 49

This technique builds on the relaxation response from the meditation, but is done when you are awake, aware, and active. As you practice the On-Demand Relaxation Technique, you'll group the body into larger segments until you can relax your entire body, mind, and energy simultaneously.

THE INNER-SMILE TECHNIQUE .... PAGE 56

This technique is designed to help you shift your body, mind, and energy to your very best life experience. Once you have programmed your Inner-Smile, all you will need to do is put the first two fingers and thumb of your non-dominant hand together to immediately be transported back to your best life experience.

> For your convenience, an audio version of the Inner-Smile Technique at the Meditative Level is available for download by following these steps:
>
> 1. Visit http://www.coachmonique.com.
>
> 2. Click the "I Bought the Book, now I need the Inner-Simile Technique Download."
>
> 3. Enter the password Iamsmiling (capital *I*, no spaces).

THE PEEL-AWAY-THE-STORY TECHNIQUE .... PAGE 67

It's what you don't know that you don't know that can hold you back in life. The five questions in this technique will help you get "in the know" and discover deep-seated beliefs that are holding you back. You'll uncover your real fears and question/challenge what you really believe you deserve or what is even possible for you.

The Setting-an-Intention Technique .... Page 78

When we focus on what we don't want, we get more of the same. This technique will guide you to shift your focus to what you do want. You'll reap the rewards.

The Heart-Centered Breathing Technique .... Page 89

This technique will guide you to use your breath and visualization to transform negative painful emotions and experience more love, peace, and happiness.

Communication Guidelines

No one technique can address all the elements of communication. If you are having issues with communication, see the following:

- ❑ Show up in productive ways .... Page 94
- ❑ Basic communication guidelines .... Page 95
- ❑ Guidelines for responding to conflict constructively .... Page 96
- ❑ Outline for setting healthy boundaries .... Page 98
- ❑ Listen to understand .... Page 101
- ❑ Learn the art of the apology .... Page 101
- ❑ Guard against defensiveness .... Page 102

The Stepping-into-the-Next-Best-Version-of-Yourself Technique .... Page 111

Setting goals, experiencing growth, and managing inevitable changes can prove challenging. This technique will guide you to have a system in place from the very beginning to deal with challenges and setback. You'll also find a guide to overcoming obstacles on page 115.

The Forgiveness Technique .... Page 126

We often refuse to forgive a person who has hurt us because we think that person doesn't deserve to be forgiven. In truth, forgiveness is a gift you give yourself so that you can break the bonds that keep you tied to a painful incident or past. This technique will show you how to forgive without condoning or erasing what has happened or necessarily restoring trust in a person who has done wrong.

Sometimes the person you need to forgive is yourself. When this is the case, review the Forgiveness Technique and the special instructions in the chapter.

Steps to Building Confidence .... Page 133

Confidence is an inside job. No matter how confident you become, you'll need to continue to build confidence. These pages will guide you in exercises to help build your overall confidence. They will also guide you through quick-and-dirty exercises for days and situations, when you need a confidence boost fast.

ABOUT THE AUTHOR

Coach Monique DeMonaco is a certified Emotional Intelligence Life Coach with an Innovation-Focused MBA from Carlow University and a BA in Communication from Chatham University. Personal experience; 20+ years of education and training; and a natural drive to do better, live better, and be better, motivates Coach Monique to coach others in their quest for positive and sustainable life change.

After growing up in rural Pennsylvania amidst struggle with undiagnosed epilepsy and significant learning disabilities, Coach Monique married and became the mother of her first son (Scott) at the age of 19. By age 21 she was a single mother. With no marketable skills, she struggled to support herself and Scott until finally realizing her lifelong dream of going to college. Shortly after graduating, Coach Monique remarried and went on to have a second son (Anso). Despite living a life she had previously only dreamed of, she found herself unhappy and angry with no real explanation—and feeling guilty and ashamed because of it. On Christmas Day in 1995, Coach Monique read a passage in a self-help book that forever changed her life. For the next 20 years, she "worked herself like a full-time job," pursing education, personal development, therapy, transformational thought training, and paradigm-shift educational programs, exploring what it meant to be happy and experience positive, sustainable change. During her journey, Coach Monique was blessed with twin boys (Zane and Henry) and became a divorced single mother again.

Realizing that she was not alone in her struggles, Coach Monique used her training and personal experience to develop easy-to-learn and easy-to-use techniques, programs, and seminars that produce rapid results. Her techniques can benefit nearly everyone, regardless of age. Today she has a thriving coaching practice, conducts workshops, provides employee development training, and enjoys motivational speaking. She is happily married to Larry, and they enjoy a busy family life: raising the boys and spending time with Larry's daughters (Kelly and Kristi) and four grandchildren (Jacob, Ollie, Maddox, and Riley).

Printed in Great Britain
by Amazon